Wellington
1936–

KEY
Books

HISTORIC MILITARY AIRCRAFT SERIES, VOLUME 35

Front cover image: Before Wellington Mk III Z1572 arrived at 419 (Moose) Squadron, the fortunate bomber had already been in action with 115 and 75 (New Zealand) Squadrons. The Wellington went on to serve 427 (Lion) Squadron and finally 16 OTU without incident until April 1945. (Charles E brown via *Aeroplane*)

Contents page image: P9249, a Wellington Mk IA captured during an air test from Weybridge in late 1939, before delivery to 38 Squadron at RAF Marham. Note the Fraser-Nash turrets minus their armament. (*Aeroplane*)

Back cover image: Vickers Warwick ASR.1, HF944 is recorded as crashing into trees at Silloth after a failed overshoot on 8 July 1946. (Via Martyn Chorlton)

Published by Key Books
An imprint of Key Publishing Ltd
PO Box 100
Stamford
Lincs PE9 1XQ

www.keypublishing.com

Original edition published as *Aeroplane's Vickers Wellington: The Backbone of Bomber Command* © 2014, edited by Martyn Chorlton

This edition © 2023

ISBN 978 1 80282 749 1

Typeset by SJmagic DESIGN SERVICES, India.

Contents

Introduction

Wellington

The Vickers Wellington is one of the world's greatest aircraft, both for its outstanding war record and operational life. However, the Wellington also played a key role in shaping Europe's bomber policy during those shaky political years that led up to the Munich crisis in 1938. Back in 1932, the restrictive Specification B.9/32 was issued for a twin-engined day bomber, to which Rex Pierson, Vickers-Armstrongs' chief designer, responded brilliantly. It was from this crucial, well-timed specification that the seeds were sown from which Bomber Command became such a powerful force that within the space of a decade, 1,000 heavy bombers could be called upon to '...reap the whirlwind' and, in the case of the first such operation against Cologne in late May 1942, more than half of the force were Wellingtons.

The father of them all, the prototype Vickers B.9/32, K4049, which first flew on 15 July 1936. Just a few days after this historic event, the Air Ministry placed an order for 180 Wellingtons; nine years later the last of 11,461 rolled off the production line. (*Aeroplane*)

The Wellington was the second aircraft (the first in RAF service was the Wellesley) to appear from the Vickers stable, which embraced a new technology – namely geodetic construction. It was in 1930 that the combined talents of Barnes Wallis and Rex Pierson came together for the first time, the latter creating the form of the new aircraft and the former implementing its structure. The resulting aircraft was a strange mix of modern, innovative construction, covered in traditional fabric, which, to the untrained eye, appeared to be far too complicated ever to reach mass production. Ironically, despite its complex appearance, Wallis's geodetics proved to be very easy to mass produce using a semi-skilled workforce, and was just as easy to repair. Nicknamed the 'basketweave bomber' by the press and the more affectionate name of 'Wimpy' by the RAF, the Wellington's construction alone would save a large number of crews following flak or fighter damage to their aircraft, which other types would never have withstood.

Even when the future policy of Bomber Command was to become an all-four-engined 'heavy' force from 1940, the Wellington stood resilient in ever-increasing numbers and continued to serve Bomber Command in the front line over Europe until its final raid in October 1943. By then, the Halifax and Lancaster had taken over as the 'backbone' while the pioneering Stirling was being prepared for withdrawal into other roles. The Wellington in the Middle Eastern, Mediterranean and Far Eastern theatres continued as one of the main offensive bombers right up to early 1945 and, in Coastal Command service, the type remained to the bitter end of the conflict and beyond.

Refined through a large number of marks, the Wellington remained in production throughout the war and continued to serve the RAF in a training role until the early 1950s. The Wellington's contribution to Britain's war effort was remarkable, from its role as a frontline bomber to its huge secondary role of serving Operational Training Units (OTUs) across the country, which continued to the end of the war; the Wimpy could always be relied on to do the job.

Chapter 1

The Geodetic 'Iron Duke'

Wellington (B.9/32 (Type 271))

It was in October 1932 that Vickers placed a tender to Specification B.9/32 for a twin-engined medium bomber. A great deal was made of the fact that the B.9/32 would make full use of geodetics, a method that had already proved itself to be the strongest method of construction being practised at the time, and it had been endorsed during structural tests by the Royal Aircraft Establishment (RAE) at Farnborough. As a result of the potential strength of the airframe alone, the Air Ministry ordered a single Type 271 prototype.

Thanks to the perseverance of Rex Pierson and Gustav Lachmann of Handley Page (who was also tendering for B.9/32), the long-held traditional method of making manufacturers stick to a tare weight laid down in the original specification was lifted from June 1934. This meant that the designers had the freedom to choose whatever powerplant was available. When the B.9/32 tender was submitted in 1933, the aircraft was to weigh 6,300lb but, by the time the prototype flew, its physical weight was 11,508lb. This freedom from weight restriction was not available to aircraft designers prior to B.9/32 and, as a result of it lifting, more appropriate aircraft began to enter service.

The B.9/32 was designed in response to world events that began in 1932 when the Geneva Conference of Disarmament sought to impose a tare weight limit of 6,500lb on all bombers. Clearly Germany and Italy had different ideas and the proposals from the conference were soon dismissed and an arms

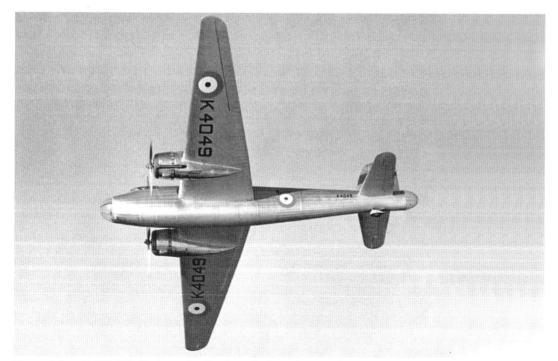

The prototype B.9/32, K4049, pictured at Hendon only days after it made its maiden flight from Brooklands on 15 June 1936. The aircraft was called the Crecy at the time of this photograph but within two months was renamed the Wellington after the first Duke of Wellington. (*Aeroplane*)

Wellington (Prototype)	
ENGINE	Two 915hp Bristol Pegasus X
WINGSPAN	86ft
LENGTH	61ft 3in
HEIGHT	17ft 5in
WING AREA	840sq/ft
EMPTY WEIGHT	18,000lb
GROSS WEIGHT	24,850lb
MAX SPEED	250mph at 8,000ft
SERVICE CEILING	21,600ft
RANGE	3,200 miles

race began. The Wellington was originally named the Crecy but was later renamed after the Duke of Wellington. It would be at the forefront of this race and would provide the backbone for a Bomber Command, which initially struggled to find its way.

Serialled K4049, the prototype B.9/32 was first flown by Mutt Summers on 15 June 1936. Within days, it was on public display at Hendon. The aircraft only bore a passing resemblance to the future Wellington since it had no turrets and a tail that was 'borrowed' from a Supermarine Stranraer flying-boat. The powerplant changed many times thanks to the looser specification and the prototype was fitted with the latest 915hp Bristol Pegasus X engines.

The aircraft was designed for a crew of four, plus room for a fifth for special duties. The potential bomb load was nine 500lb bombs or nine 250lb bombs for long-range operations. Although not fitted, defensive armament would have been light with a single .303in machine gun in the nose and another in the tail.

Declared as one of the most advanced aircraft of the day and backed up by excellent test reports from the Aeroplane and Armament Experimental Establishment (A&AEE), an order was placed for 180 Mk Is in 1935. However, the full flight programme of prototype K4049 was destined never to be completed as the aircraft was lost on 19 April 1937 after a horn balance failed over Brightwell in Suffolk. The pilot was thrown clear as the bomber turned on to its back. The only other occupant, the flight engineer, was unable to escape before the aircraft hit the ground.

Wellington Mk II – Merlin-powered blockbuster

The design of the Wellington Mk II began in January 1938 with the Rolls-Royce Merlin X engine. The change of powerplant would enable production of the aircraft to remain uninterrupted if the supply of the existing Pegasus should fail through technical problems or, more likely, enemy action.

The Mk II would not be available until 1939. It was fitted with Frazer-Nash gun turrets and a 24V electrical system was installed for both aircraft and radio services. The hydraulic system was upgraded with VSG-type pumps, which supplied up to 1,000lb/sq in power supply for all aircraft services plus 300lb/sq into a secondary system that powered the gun turrets. The oxygen system was also modified to suit the Frazer-Nash turrets. All of these upgrades were incorporated into the Mk IA and IC before the Mk II even flew.

By early 1939, the Merlin X engine was ready for testing and, on 3 March 1939, the Mk II prototype, L4250, made its maiden flight from Brooklands. The Merlins were more than 100hp more powerful than the Pegasus but, being water-cooled, were much heavier; the Mk II weighed 4,500lbs more than the

A pre-delivery photograph of Mk II, W5379, before it was despatched to 12 Squadron at Binbrook, Lincolnshire in November 1940. The bomber crashed near Haamstede in the Netherlands during a raid to Cologne on 11 October 1941. (Via Martyn Chorlton)

Mk IC. However, the Mk II could fly higher and faster but at the price of a lower bomb load and shorter maximum range.

This did not stop the Mk II being the first Wellington to be converted to carry the Barnes Wallis-designed 4,000lb 'Blockbuster' bomb following modifications to the bomb bay. Production aircraft also incorporated long-range fuel tanks and tropicalisation, which would see the aircraft's all-up weight increase to 33,000lb.

The Wellington Mk II first entered service with 12 Sqn and 142 Sqn at Binbrook, Lincolnshire, in November 1940. It later joined 9, 38, 57, 99, 104, 148, 158, 214, 218, 305, 405 and 466 Squadrons. The first

Wellington Mk II	
ENGINE	Two 1,145hp Rolls-Royce Merlin X
WINGSPAN	86ft 2in
LENGTH	64ft 7in
HEIGHT	17ft 5in
WING AREA	840sq/ft
EMPTY WEIGHT	20,258lb
GROSS WEIGHT	33,000lb
MAX SPEED	254mph at 17,500ft
SERVICE CEILING	23,500ft

delivery of the effective 4,000lb bomb was carried out by a Mk II over Emden, northern Germany, on 1 April 1941; the weapon having been approved by the Ministry of Aircraft Production (MAP) in March.

Two prototypes, L4250 and T2545, plus 399 Mk IIs were built in two main batches of 199 (in the range W5352 to W5611) and 200 (in the range Z8328 to Z8662) under the same contract number B.7144/40 all at Weybridge, Surrey.

Wellington Mk III – Hercules-powered 'Wimpy'

The Wellington Mk III followed a similar path in its development, since it was also designed with an alternative powerplant; this time the Bristol Hercules. Orders to proceed with Mk II and III were issued simultaneously, with the intention of converting the tenth and eleventh aircraft from first production but, because of delays with both engines, the 38th and 39th aircraft were eventually selected.

The first of two Mk III prototypes, L4251, was flown with Hercules HEISM engines on 19 May 1939 with Summers at the controls, R C Handasyde as flight test observer, and Wg Cdr Rider-Young as the sole crewmember. The HEISM was a twin-stage supercharged engine fitted with a 12ft 6in diameter de Havilland constant-speed propeller.

Early flight trials proved disappointing and the expected superior performance over the Mk I was lacking so the aircraft was sent to Bristol for further development work. A second aircraft, ex-Mk IC P9238, was also converted to Mk III standard with Hercules III engines. Fitted with a Rotol electric propeller, the second aircraft, after its maiden flight in January 1941, performed closer to expectations and was selected as the first production Mk III. Mk IIIs introduced a new rear FN20 rear turret with a much more effective quartet of .303in machine guns and de-icing equipment. Like the Mk II, the Mk III had tropical equipment including long-range fuel tanks and air filters over the engine intakes fitted on the production line making the type ideal for quickly re-equipping squadrons in the Middle East.

The prototype Mk III, L4251, which was actually the 39th production Mk I pictured at Boscombe Down during trials with the Aeroplane & Armament Experimental Establishment (A&AEE). (Via Martyn Chorlton)

Wellington Mk III	
ENGINE	Two 1,590hp Bristol Hercules HEISM or two Hercules III
WINGSPAN	86ft 2in
LENGTH	64ft 7in
HEIGHT	17ft 5in
WING AREA	840sq/ft
EMPTY WEIGHT	18,000lb
GROSS WEIGHT	28,500lb
MAX SPEED	255mph at 15,000ft
SERVICE CEILING	18,000ft
RANGE	2,200 miles with 1,500lb bomb load and 1,540 miles with 4,500lb bomb load

The Mk III did not enter Bomber Command service until June 1941 but would prove to be the mainstay until the re-equipment with the four-engined heavies began to gain momentum. The Mk III served with 9, 12, 37, 40, 57, 70, 75, 99, 101, 115, 142, 150, 156, 162, 166, 192, 196, 199, 300, 419, 420, 424, 425, 426, 427, 428 & 429 Squadrons and was withdrawn from Bomber Command frontline service in October 1943, and continued to serve with the Operational Training Units (OTU) until the end of the war.

A total of 1,519 Mk IIIs were built; 780 of them at Blackpool, 737 at Chester and the two prototypes, L4251 and P9238 at Weybridge.

Wellington Mk IV – More airframes than engines

By the beginning of the World War Two, the rate at which Wellington airframes were being produced exceeded engine production by a considerable margin. The amount of liquid-cooled Merlin engines available also reduced as these were being diverted to fighter aircraft production. The only option was to look overseas and, while the US aircraft industry was the first choice, Alfa Romeo was considered because at this stage of the war, Italy was neutral.

The prototype Mk IV, R1220, was drawn from the Mk IC production line along with the next 24 aircraft built. The aircraft initially suffered from vibration problems after its maiden flight in December 1940, which were cured by fitting a pair of Curtiss electric propellers.

Wellington Mk IV	
ENGINE	Two 1,050hp Twin Wasp R-183S3C4-C
WINGSPAN	86ft 2in
LENGTH	64ft 7in
HEIGHT	17ft 5in
WING AREA	840sq/ft
GROSS WEIGHT	31,500lb
MAX SPEED	255mph at 15,000ft
SERVICE CEILING	18,000ft
RANGE	1,500 miles

On 9 September 1939, a contract was placed with the American manufacturer, Pratt & Whitney (P&W), for a pair of its Twin Wasp SC3-9 engines to be fitted to a single prototype. By February 1940, the US government had given permission for the more powerful R-2800 to be made available to the British. The R-2800 was a heavier power plant equal in power to the planned Hercules-powered version of the Wellington. After Rex Pierson made a request to the Air Ministry for the R-2800, the reply was that the Curtiss Wright Cyclone GR-1820/C2054 had been selected, but this option was also later cancelled.

After a period of indecision, the apparent imminent invasion of Britain in July 1940 realigned priorities and the option of American engines was looked at again. On 27 July, a decision was made to install the 1,050hp P&W Twin Wasp R-183S3C4-C engine into the Wellington, which would become the Mk IV. All other systems of the Mk IV were little different from the Mk IC and performance figures compared to the Mk III.

Just four months after instructions to proceed were received from the Air Ministry, the first Twin Wasp-powered Mk IV, R1220, made its maiden flight from Hawarden, Wales, in the hands of Maurice Hare in December 1940. All Mk IV production would subsequently be carried out at Chester and the first of 220 aircraft built began to enter service from August 1941. The Wellington Mk IV served with 142, 300, 301, 305, 458, 460 and 544 Squadrons continuing in Bomber Command's frontline operations until March 1943.

The 220 Mk IVs were made up of the prototype, ex-Mk IC, R1220, plus 24 others drawn from the same Mk IC batch. The main contract for 195 new-build Mk IVs placed to Contract B97887/40 were in the serial ranges Z1182 and Z1183, Z1202 to Z1292, Z1311 to Z1345 and Z1375 to Z1496. This entire batch was delivered between June 1941 and March 1942.

Wellington Mk X – The most prolific Wimpy of all

By the time the development of the Wellington had reached the Mk III stage, the aircraft had reached its maximum loading. Further development of the type seemed unlikely until a new light alloy was produced with a much higher load capacity. When the new alloy was made available to Vickers, the Wellington was given a new lease of life.

Incorporating the new alloy into the structure for the Wellington caused very few problems but allowed the aircraft to have a much greater all-up weight without increasing the weight of the airframe itself. The opportunity was also taken to install the high-powered 1,675hp Bristol Hercules VI or XVI engines.

To test the new engines, Mk III, X3374, was trialled as the Mk X prototype, powered by a pair of Hercules VI engines. By July 1942, the first production Type 440 Mk X, DF609, left the Blackpool

The Mk X represented the pinnacle of development of the Wellington in the bomber role but, from this mark, a host of other Coastal Command and trainer variants would evolve. This is Blackpool-built HZ470, which, after serving with 424 and 429 Squadrons and 83 OTU, is pictured during its final tour of RAF duty with 86 OTU out of Gamston.

production line, a few weeks behind schedule. All Mk X production was subsequently shared between Blackpool and Chester, HE147 being the first to be built at the latter.

The Mk X was destined to have a short career on the frontline with Bomber Command, the type arrived in December 1942 with 431 Sqn at Burn, North Yorkshire. By October 1943, the Mk X had been withdrawn from Bomber Command in favour of the four-engined heavies. The Mk X quickly took over all of the roles of the Mk III, its improved performance and reliability being appreciated by its crews.

The Mk X remained in front line service in the RAF, performing general duties in many theatres and was retained in the bomber role in the Middle East, North Africa and India until the end of the

Wellington X	
ENGINE	Two 1,675hp Hercules VI/XVI
WINGSPAN	86ft 2in
LENGTH	64ft 7in
HEIGHT	17ft 6in
WING AREA	840sq/ft
EMPTY WEIGHT	22,474lb
GROSS WEIGHT	36,500lb
MAX SPEED	255mph
SERVICE CEILING	22,000ft
RANGE	1,885 miles at 180 mph with 1,500lb bomb load

war, serving with operational squadrons. These were 36, 37, 40, 70, 99, 104, 142, 150, 162, 166, 192, 196, 199, 215, 300, 304, 305, 420, 424, 425, 426, 427, 428, 429. The abundance of Mk Xs meant that the hard-pressed bomber OTUs were re-equipped with the type, many of them retaining the aircraft into the immediate post-war period. Many Mk Xs were converted into trainers and this type proved most adaptable as an engine test-bed including one aircraft (a T Mk X), LN715, which carried out sterling work in the development of the Rolls-Royce Dart turboprop.

In total, 3,803 Mk Xs were built at Blackpool and Chester from 1942 to 25 October 1945, when the last aircraft, RP590, was delivered to the RAF from Blackpool.

Wellington GR Mk XI, XII, XIII and XIV – Hercules-powered General Reconnaissance variants of the Wimpy

The outstanding design of the Mk X airframe would provide the basis for many variants of the Wellington family, including the General Reconnaissance (GR) types, which served Coastal Command from late 1942 to the end of the war.

The first of the four variants that used the Mk X airframe was GR Mk XI, which was similar to its older sibling, only differing in having a Type 454 ASW Mk II radar fitted, a retractable Leigh under the rear fuselage and the provision to carry a pair of 18in torpedoes. Introduced in January 1943, the Mk XI was followed by the Mk XII. The main difference between the Mk XII and the previous mark was the radar, which was now the ASV Mk III. This differed from the older Mk II by being contained within a teardrop fairing under the chin of the bomber while the previous system relied on numerous external aerials. The new radar equipment forced the removal of the front turret, which initially made the aircraft vulnerable

GR MK XIV, MP714, pictured during rocket projectile (RP) trials with the A&AEE out of Boscombe Down in 1943. The aircraft later served with 612 and 179 Squadrons and finally 6 OTU at Kinloss. It was finally struck off charge (SOC) on 27 March 1943.

Wellington GR Mk XI, XII, XVII and XIV	
ENGINE	(XI and XII) Two 1,675hp Hercules VI/XVI; (XVII and XIV) two 1,735hp Hercules XVII
WINGSPAN	86ft 2in
LENGTH	64ft 7in
HEIGHT	17ft 5in
WING AREA	840sq/ft
EMPTY WEIGHT	22,474lb
GROSS WEIGHT	36,500lb
MAX SPEED	255mph
SERVICE CEILING	22,000ft
RANGE	1,885 miles at 180mph with 1,500lb bomb load

to attack from a U-boat that was prepared to fight it out on the surface. A pair of Browning machine guns on flexible mounts was later installed in the Mk XIIs.

The GR Mk XIII and the GR Mk XIV were both fitted with 1,735hp Hercules XVII engines and Leigh Lights. The Mk XIII served as a torpedo bomber with ASV Mk II radar while the Mk XIV served in the anti-submarine role and was fitted with ASV Mk III radar and some were operated with radar processing on rails mounted outboard of the engines and depth charges.

GR Mk XI was the second of the Mk X GR sub-variants to enter service when it was delivered to 407 Squadron at Docking, Norfolk, in January 1943. While the type's service with 407 Squadron was short, six other units were equipped with the mark, the last, 344 Squadron at Dakar, Senegal, did not retire theirs until November 1945.

The GR Mk XII was the first of the new generation of Coastal Command Wellingtons to enter service when it joined 172 Squadron at Chivenor in December 1942. The type did not enjoy a long service career and was withdrawn by February 1944. The GR Mk XIII was the most used of the three variants; the Wellington served with 17 Coastal Command squadrons from July 1943 right through to April 1946 when the type was retired by 294 Squadron at Idku, Egypt.

The final variant, the GR Mk XIV, served with 11 RAF squadrons from June 1943 to December 1946. The type was first issued to the auxiliary unit, 612 (County of Aberdeen) Squadron at Chivenor, Devon, and was retired by 38 Squadron at Grottaglie, Southern Italy.

The maritime-type Wellingtons were used extensively by Coastal Command as well as overseas. Their contribution was outstanding and their involvement in the war against the U-boat resulted in 26 enemy submarines being sunk and many more being damaged by Wellingtons.

180 GR Mk XI, 58 GR Mk XII, 844 GR Mk XIII and GR Mk 841 XIVs were built between 1943 and 1945.

Wellington T Mk XVII, XVIII, X and XIX – The Wimpy 'flying classrooms'

The dedicated purpose-built Wellington trainer was a long time coming, simply because the early marks were fitted with dual controls which made pilot training a lot easier. These were coupled to the main controls and were mounted on a floor extension positioned forward of the starboard seat.

As specialist training OTUs (Operational Training Units) began to form in numbers during the early stages of the war, many ex-operational Wellingtons were handed down to these units and many more

By far the most prolifically produced of the Wellington trainers, the type was the last example of the pre-bomber to see RAF service when it was retired in March 1953. RP589 is pictured at Brooklands in January 1949.

One of 80 new build T Mk XVIIIs built between May and October 1945 by Vickers at Blackpool was RP413. The aircraft only served until it was SOC on 1 April 1952.

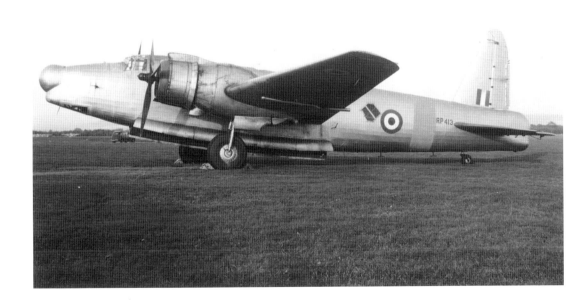

Wellington T Mk X	
ENGINE	Two 1,675hp Hercules VI/XVI
WINGSPAN	86ft 2in
LENGTH	64ft 7in
HEIGHT	17ft 6in
WING AREA	840sq/ft
EMPTY WEIGHT	22,474lb
GROSS WEIGHT	36,500lb
MAX SPEED	255mph
SERVICE CEILING	22,000ft
RANGE	2,000 miles

were converted with dual controls. As more specialist training was required and the amount of surplus Wellingtons began to increase, the type found itself being converted into navigation, radio operator and airborne interception (AI) training aircraft.

In numerical order, the first of the main trainer variants was the T Mk XVII which was converted from ex-Hercules XVII-powered GR Mk XI Coastal Command Wellingtons. The aircraft was modified to train night fighter crews and the nose turret was replaced by a Mosquito-type SCR 720 AI radar set. The rear turret was also removed from the first purpose-built Wellington 'flying classroom'.

The next Wellington trainer was the T Mk XVIII which was a conversion of the B Mk X and GR Mk XIII and was also employed to train radar operators. Equipped as per the T Mk XVII, the aircraft had room for four pupils and an instructor. All of the conversion work for this mark was carried out at Blackpool where a large number of new-build aircraft were also produced.

A large number of B Mk Xs were converted by Boulton Paul at Wolverhampton into dual-control T Mk Xs during the post-war period. The airframes were completely stripped, overhauled and recovered and fully fitted out as Navigation trainers. Once again, both the nose and rear turrets were removed and faired over.

Nine T Mk XVII were converted from GR Mk XIs; 80 T Mk XVIII were converted at Blackpool from GR Mk XIIIs and 270 ex-B Mk Xs were converted to T Mk X (T.10) trainers by Boulton Paul between January 1946 and March 20, 1952. An unknown number of B Mk X airframes were converted by the RAF to T Mk XIX standard.

Wellington C Mk IX, XV and XVI – The Wimpy Transports

From the outset, the concept of utilising the Wellington as a civilian or military transport aircraft was considered but, despite several proposals being put forward before the outbreak of World War Two, none came to fruition. Several Wellington Mk Is were converted 'ad hoc' as passenger-carrying aircraft, usually for bespoke specialist operations, rather than as a production run. However, in 1941, the Air Ministry asked Vickers to begin preparing technical information for a freight and/or troop-carrying variant of the Wellington. At the same time, a high-priority request was issued by the RAF's Middle East Command for transport aircraft to increase the mobility of forces in the region.

The request, at first, involved a basic conversion of the Wellington bomber to transport troops and their equipment by removing all unnecessary military equipment. This included the space-consuming oxygen equipment to make way for seats, which were of a similar pattern to those fitted into the pre-war Valentia.

Having already served with the New Zealand Flight (as NZ502) and 15 and 27 OTUs, ex-Wellington Mk I was converted to a C Mk I, and reverted to its original production serial L4340 when it served with 24 Squadron at Hendon. Named the *Duke of Rutland*, the aircraft served until November 1944.

Aircraft converted were ex-Mk ICs, IIs, IIIs and IVs and the transformation from a bomber was carried out at RAF stations across the globe; as a result, the number of Wellingtons that were changed to this more passive role is unknown.

As demand grew for transport aircraft, Vickers began converting much larger numbers, especially as more ex-Bomber Command Mk I, IA and IC variants became available. At least 100 Mk ICs were converted, which finally justified the type having a proper designation and, from 1943, the aircraft were referred to as the C Mk IA and C Mk IC. However, this designation, which would become more familiar to transport aircraft during the post-war years, was dropped in favour of the C Mk XV and C Mk XVI respectively.

The entire range of transport aircraft was encompassed by the Type 437 Wellington Mk IX, which could carry 18 fully equipped troops at a range of between 1,000 and 2,000 miles depending on the load being carried.

Little is recorded regarding which aircraft served with which units and only the brief service of the C Mk XVI is known. This mark first joined 24 Squadron at Hendon, north London, in February 1943 but was retired by January 1944. It did not reappear in the records until 232 and 242 Squadrons were reformed at Stoney Cross, in the heart of the New Forest, on 15 November 1944. 232 Squadron received its first aircraft in December 1944 but had retired them in favour of the Liberator Mk VII in February 1945, while 242 Squadron received its first C Mk XVI in January 1945 but only them kept them a few weeks before they were replaced by the much larger Stirling Mk V.

Wellington C Mk IX, XV and XVI	
ENGINE	(XVI) Two 1,050hp Bristol Pegasus XVIII
WINGSPAN	86ft 2in
LENGTH	64ft 7in
HEIGHT	17ft 5in
WING AREA	840 sq/ft
MAX SPEED	235mph at 10,000ft
RANGE	(IX) 1,000 to 2,000 miles

One of 50 Wellington Mk ICs built by Vickers at Weybridge and delivered between March and April 1940, P9249 was allocated to 38 Squadron stationed at Marham. The aircraft lost an engine on take-off from Marham for a ferry flight, struck a water tank and was written off. (*Aeroplane*)

Chapter 2

1650 Geodetic Segments

From a period article dated 5 July 1939 and published in *The Aeroplane* magazine:

Vickers-Armstrongs' Wellingtons are now being supplied to the RAF in very large numbers at a high rate of weekly output. This is not only the result of the enormous scope of Vickers-Armstrongs' resources, but is primarily because of the skilful way in which the geodetic construction has been adapted to modern methods of production.

Geodetic construction was primarily devised as the most efficient method of disposing the structural material within the lines of a finely streamlined modern aircraft – that is, to get the lightest possible structure for a cantilever monoplane of high-aspect ratio. The achievement of this goal has been convincingly demonstrated by the performance of the Vickers-Armstrongs' Wellesley monoplanes, two of which hold the present World's Distance Record of 7,162 miles.

The Wellingtons, as the immediate successors of these record-breaking machines, naturally profit by the structural efficiency of geodetic construction. This is made amply clear by the good ratio of tare to maximum permissible loaded weight (16,600–27,000lb).

A Vickers Wellington Mk I with two 965hp Bristol Pegasus XVIII motors, just off the production line at Weybridge, during flying trials. (*Aeroplane*)

The set of six fuel tanks ready to be slid within the wing. A wing can be taken off, the tanks changed and the wing replaced within two and half hours. (*Aeroplane*)

This excellent result has been achieved in a machine that has a top speed of 265mph at 17,700ft on two Bristol Pegasus XVIII motors. Even finer performances have been achieved on later models that have two 1,075hp Rolls-Royce Merlins or two 1,375hp Bristol Hercules motors. The actual figures have not yet been released. These performances illustrate the high aerodynamic efficiency of the Wellington as designed by Mr Rex Pierson and his staff.

The notable ratio of empty to loaded weight means that the Wellington has remarkably long ranges for heavy service loads. This valuable feature is further enhanced by the high aspect ratio made economically possible by geodetic construction. This reduces the induced drag and consequently lowers the power required for cruising – or makes possible a higher cruising speed for a given power.

The standard cruising speed is 215mph at 15,000ft and the maximum range 3,200 miles at an economical cruising speed of 180mph. Performances such as these, officially recognised, appear to justify the belief that a Wellington, tanked up for a long-range flight, should be able to do about 10,000 miles non-stop.

A weapon of great importance

Strategically, the Wellington must be a weapon of very great importance to the RAF. A range of 3,000 miles means that all possible objectives can be reached from British bases across the world. And the Wellingtons can take themselves to such bases without undesirable halts for refuelling.

From the aerodynamic standpoint, the layout of the Wellington is good. The fuselage, in spite of having heavily armed gun-turrets in the nose and tail, is clean. The narrow tapering wings with the high aspect

The main spar floats freely through the fuselage, connects loads between wings and fuselage being transferred by front and rear spars via a heavy root rib, which is bolted to the main fuselage frames. This is the front spar attachment. (Vickers via *Aeroplane*)

ratio of 8.83 made economically possible by geodetic construction are in the mid-wing position so that there is the minimum interference between them and the sides of the fuselage. The Wellington usually carries five men. In the nose is the front gunner's station, below him the bomb-aimer's position. Behind on the port side is the single pilot's seat with only one set of controls. On a higher level, behind the pilot and over the bomb-beams, are positions for the radio operator and navigator. There is a transparent cupola in the roof through which the latter can take sights. There is also an ingenious arrangement of hinged arms whereby the navigator can make himself fast (in the nautical sense). In the extreme tail is the aft gun-station.

Careful attention has been paid to the comfort of the crew. The incoming fresh air can be heated at will by the well-known Gallay system. Steam is raised in a boiler around the exhaust pipe of the port motor. It is fed to a heater in the fresh air duct. The walls of the cabin are sound-proofed.

The flying qualities of the Wellington are remarkable for so large an aircraft. Those of us who were lucky enough to attend the Garden Party of the Royal Aeronautical Society at the beginning of the summer were much impressed by the way in which this big bomber was handled during its demonstration by Flt Lt M F Summers (RAF Oman). Not only was its high turn of speed convincingly shown off, but its qualities of manoeuvrability and general handiness were most impressive.

Before describing the interesting processes whereby the Wellingtons are being turned out in such large quantities at Weybridge, we will describe the structure of the machine in detail.

The Wings

The wings are built in three parts; the wings proper and the centre section. The former carry the Frise ailerons and split trailing-edge flaps. Both wings and the centre section are built on the geodetic principle.

A geodetic line is the shortest distance between two points on a curved surface. And the principle on which geodetic construction is based is to provide a structure, the members of which shall carry the loads through the shortest possible paths. In a wing, for instance, the bending loads, that is, the loads that tend to deflect the wing up or down, are taken by a girder spar – the best way of doing that job. In the Wellington, this spar consists of main booms made up of Duralumin tubes, linked by diagonals of special section rolled from strip.

One of the features of the Vickers geodetic construction is the use of very thick-walled tubes. This design feature is based on results obtained from a very large number of experiments done in the laboratories at Weybridge to determine the best ratio between the diameter of a tube and the thickness of its wall. If the latter becomes less than a certain proportion of the diameter, the tube will fail by buckling and so not carry the load it should have been able to carry if the strength of the material were properly used.

In the wings of the Wellington, all the torsion loads, that is loads that tend to twist the wing, are taken by geodetic members. These members are rolled to a special section so designed that the material, Duralumin, will develop its full strength without failure through secondary causes such as buckling. Obviously, this is what every designer tries to do. Nevertheless, the various tests made on full-size geodetic components, such as wings, have shown that geodetic construction is extraordinarily successful in developing the full strength of the structural material.

A feature of geodetic construction is that the criss-crossing geodetic members are self-stabilising. One might imagine that the application of a load would tend to pull or squash the curved geodetic members flat, but this is not so. Any force that tends to force one set of geodetic members outwards or inwards, is exactly balanced by an opposite force in the intersecting set.

Consequently, no ribs are needed to keep the wing to its proper shape. The curved shape of each geodetic member is worked out in the drawing office to give the appropriate contour to the wing of fuselage.

In the Wellington, the geodetic members of the upper and lower surfaces are linked by auxiliary spars close to the leading and trailing edges. These spars, in conjunction with the geodetics, carry the drag and anti-drag loads.

The centre-section is built in the same general style except that the main girder-spar is in halves so that it may be joined after being put into place in the fuselage. The wings are joined to the centre-section through the medium of the nacelles. This will be explained when the nacelles are described.

The method of joining the wings to the fuselage is particularly interesting. There are no ribs inside the wings, though there are master-ribs where the centre-section meets the fuselage and at the roots of the wings themselves. The girder-spar of the centre-section passes right through slots in the sides of the fuselage and is quite free in these.

The spar is fastened to the master-rib to which are also fastened all the geodetic members of the upper and lower surfaces. Each end of the master-rib is linked through hinge-pins to stirrup fittings on the fuselage. In this way, the wing is fixed in relation to the fuselage so far as up and down movement is concerned but is free to move backwards or forwards. It is prevented from doing this by the fillet, which is fixed to the geodetic members of the fuselage and to the master-rib.

All the surfaces are covered with fabric. This is applied in panels before the wings are assembled. It is laid on a special form of fabric beading glued on to the geodetic members. It is held on this beading by wires or by sewing according to the loads at that particular place.

The fuselage

The fuselage is likewise built on the geodetic principle. There are six main frames, two of which are comparatively light rings, one immediately in front of, and one behind, the pilot's position. Besides these two, there are two main frames to carry the attachment and two frames, which are linked together, to carry the tail unit.

The geodetic members of the fuselage are built as long panels on longitudinal tubes or longerons. After the complete fuselage has been built up, it is covered with fabric fastened to it in the same way as the covering on the wings.

The tail unit

The fin and tail-plane are cantilevers. They are built in the same manner as the wings. The tips of each are covered with metal instead of with fabric, as are the rest of the surfaces. The rudder and elevators are covered with fabric. Trimming tabs, controllable from the cockpit, are provided in both rudder and elevators.

The undercarriage

The front wheels, suspended between Vickers oleo shock-absorbers, retract backwards into the motor-nacelles. The operation is by a Vickers hydraulic jack and the mechanism noticeably straightforward. Incorporated in the system are spring-loaded pins to lock the undercarriage down. These are provided with electrical contacts, which only close the circuit to the signalling lamp when the pins are actually home.

A completely independent hydraulic system is provided for emergency actuation of the gear. The tail-wheel retracts within the fuselage and is actuated by a Vickers hydraulic jack.

Power Plant

The Vickers-Armstrongs Wellington Mk I is driven by two Bristol Pegasus XVIII air-cooled radial motors with two-speed superchargers. These provide a total of 1,930hp for take-off and a total of 1,770hp for level flight at 15,500ft. The total cruising output is 1,090hp.

The standard Pegasus nacelles will take the Rolls-Royce Merlin liquid-cooled 12-cylinder vee or the Bristol Hercules twin-row 14-cylinder sleeve-valve air-cooled radial without major alteration. The nacelles are mounted at the junction between the wings and centre section. The main girder-spar passes right through each nacelle. Provision is also made for suitable joints between the front and back auxiliary spars.

The master-ribs at the outer ends of the centre section and at the roots of the wings are linked to their appropriate nacelles through spring-loaded taper-ended screws that pick up fittings in the sides of the nacelle.

In each nacelle there is a collector tank of 55-gallons capacity for the fuel and an oil tank of 16-gallons.

One of the special features of the geodetic wing is its unobstructed interior. Full use of this is made in the Wellington. There are six tanks in each wing. The total capacity with nacelle tanks is 750 gallons. The tanks are joined together in trains of three; three in the leading edge in front of the spar, three behind it. Each train of three tanks is so connected and piped together that it can be slid in on runners.

The train is held in place with spring-loaded tapered screws of the type used to fasten the master-ribs to the nacelles. These screws can be fastened from outside the wing, consequently, the tanks can be taken out and replaced with remarkable speed.

A day or two before one visited the works recently; the tanks had to be changed in a Wellington, which was doing its flying trials. The wing was taken off, the tanks taken out, a new train of tanks put in and the wing put back, all within two and a half hours.

The ability to carry fuel in the wings, where the weight of the tanks and their contents are directly taken by the lift on the wings, is a very large contribution to structural efficiency. In this way, much weight can be saved in such members as spars, which would have to carry much larger loads if the fuel were carried in the fuselage. How large these loads might be is shown by the fact that the fuel for 3,000 miles, 1,000 gallons, weighs by 7.5 = 7,500lb or 3½ tons. This extra 250 gallons is carried in long-range tanks hung on the bomb-beams.

Turning them out

After looking at Mr Clark's drawings of the Wellington with its multitude of intersecting geodetic members, one might get the idea that geodetic bombers would be difficult to turn out in large numbers at high speed. A visit to Weybridge shows otherwise. In fact, the major components of a Wellington, apart from such things as aero-motors, airscrews, fuel tanks, wheels and the rest, seem to consist mostly of parts rolled from Duralumin strip between three and four inches wide and of specially extruded tubes of Duralumin about three inches in diameter.

A particularly interesting device has been evolved to check the thickness of the walls of these tubes, as the outsides of the tubes have to be turned true to the bore to within two-thousandths of an inch. The gauging device consists of an engineer's level mounted at the end of a long bed on which the Duralumin tube lies within a number of collars. The latter are provided with four screws each so that the tube can be centred properly within them to ensure that the bore of the tube is true to the outside of the collar. This is done by sighting the level down the bore of the tube on an illuminated grid mounted on the end of a long rod, which can be pushed down the bore of the tube.

While the tubes are being thus prepared and then machined to the limits mentioned, the geodetic members are being rolled out of strip. There are about 1,650 separate geodetic members in each Wellington. They are all of the same section but the gauges vary from 12 to 22 S.W.G.

The rolling of the geodetic members is done on a special type of rolling mill patented by Vickers. The number of stands, that is pairs of rolls, varies from five to seven. The special feature is that the sections have to be rolled with a pre-determined curvature. This is calculated in the drawing office. It is obtained by moving the last two stands of rolls while the strip is coming through. This is done by an arrangement of cams.

After the members have been rolled and cut to length, they go along to the plate jigs. As the name implies, these consist of steel plates on which the lines of a number of members have been laid out. Holes are drilled in these lines to take stirrup fittings into which the newly rolled members are clamped. The advantage of this scheme is that one plate can be marked out for a number of different members and the same stirrups will do for the lot by the simple process of placing them in the various different holes.

Expert fabric workers pictured covering a geodetic panel. (Vickers via *Aeroplane*)

While in these jigs, the members are drilled. The next operation is to make indentations to take the little butterfly pressings that join the members together, but before these are riveted in place the members have to be notched at the various intersection points. At present rates of production, a mile and a half of the extruded section from which these butterflies are pressed is being used every week.

After these butterflies have been riveted in place at the intersections, the ends of each member are notched to take the 'wish-bone' fitting, which picks up either the longitudinal tubular members of the fuselage or the tubular booms of the main or auxiliary spars of the wings.

When the geodetic members leave this department, they are ready for assembly into panels for the fuselage or wing. The panels are built in jigs, but whether for wings or fuselage, the geodetics are assembled on to master tubes at their boundary edges. This is to ensure absolute interchangeability. These master tubes are part of the jigs.

The assembly of these panels is rather easier than putting a Meccano model together as the criss-crossing members are merely laid so that they intersect at the notches with the butterfly fittings. These are so designed that a single bolt can be dropped through the axes of both butterflies to hold the crossing members in their correct position.

Gusset-plates go over the top and are riveted in place. We were interested to notice that the gusset-plates are painted in various distinctive colours according to their gauges to simplify the selection of the appropriate gusset for any joint.

After the wing panels have been assembled in this fashion they go off to be covered.

Crackers

Meanwhile, the main spars are being built. Here again the cardinal principle of unit assembly has been adopted. The diagonal bracing is built up on jigs but without the tubular booms, again to ensure absolute interchangeability. When the unit is withdrawn it looks very much like a Chinese cracker and is known as such throughout the works. The tubular booms to which we have referred are then fixed in place.

The auxiliary spars are also coming along. The construction of these is interesting. The booms, made from strip, are rolled into a circular section but not quite closed so that rivets can be readily inserted through the opposite wall to fasten the section to the web of Duralumin sheet.

In the assembly of the wings no jigs are used. This is possible because of the very close tolerances to which the unit assembly has been done. The panels, which have now been covered with fabric, are attached to the main girder spar and then auxiliary spars are added at the leading and trailing edges. The leading-edge box is added. In the way of the split flaps along the trailing edge, a tubular superstructure is added to take the fabric back to the trailing edge or in the way of the ailerons a light structure is added to take the necessary shrouding.

The wings then go to the dope shop to be doped and shadow-painted. Before this, and during assembly, all the necessary wiring and piping has been built into place.

Meantime, the fuselages have been going together. There are something like 11 major panels in each fuselage and they are put together in a jig. Each fuselage is only in a jig for 24 hours. At the end of that time, it is taken out and put into place in the assembly line in the big shed.

The machines travel up this shop tail first so that when ready they can be pushed into the flight shed without turning.

Chapter 3

Wellington Production

The most highly produced British bomber of World War Two, the Wellington, was only surpassed in the world by the B-24 Liberator and B-27 Flying Fortress. The type remained in continuous production from 1938 through to October 1945 and, such was the demand that three Vickers-controlled factories were building the type. The home of Vickers at Weybridge produced 2,515; the Squires Gate, Blackpool factory built 3,406; while Hawarden/Broughton produced 5,540 making a grand total of 11,461 Wellingtons. The most prolific of all was the Mk X, which made up 3,803 of the total and, along with the T Mk XVIII, were last to roll off the lines in October 1945.

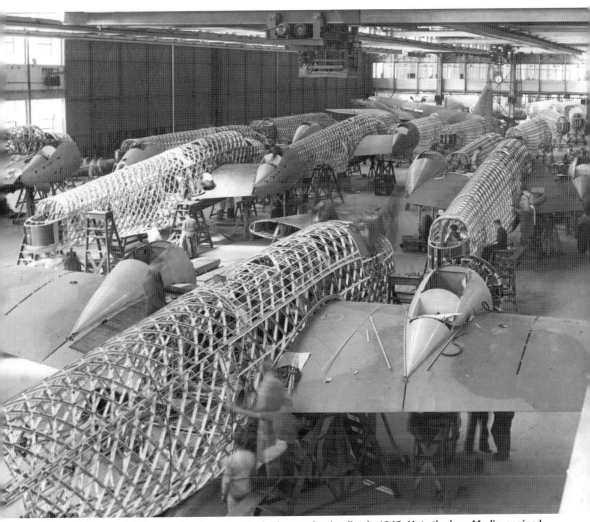

Vickers Wellington Mk Is meander down the Weybridge production line in 1940. Note the lone Merlin-engined Mk II in the background. (*Aeroplane*)

At least 14 early Wellingtons, in various stages of construction, are visible in this view of the Weybridge erecting shop in 1938. The glazed nose section and single .303in machine gun give these aircraft away as the Mk I, of which 176 were built at Weybridge. (*Aeroplane*)

Barnes Wallis's geodetic design can be fully appreciated in this view of a trio of Mk Is at Weybridge. Complex on the surface, the geodetics, once mastered by a semi-skilled workforce, could be assembled very quickly. (*Aeroplane*)

The erecting shop at Squires Gate, Blackpool, in 1944 presents a view of Mk Xs on the left and Mk XIVs on the right. In total, 1,369 Mk Xs and 249 Mk XIVs were built at Blackpool out of a total of 3,406 Wellingtons. (Vickers via *Aeroplane*)

The production numbers for the Wellington beggar belief even today and, prior to the outbreak of World War Two, one Wimpy left the Weybridge line every day. At its peak, in 1942, Wellington production saw monthly rates at Weybridge of 70 aircraft, 102 at Blackpool and 130 from Chester. (Via *Aeroplane*)

Contracts, numbers, serials and delivery dates

- Wellington (Type 271) prototype, K4049, first flew on 15 June 1936; ordered to the specification B.9/32 under Contract 274142/33 by Vickers, Weybridge. Delivered to Royal Aircraft Establishment (RAE) in September 1936 and the Aeroplane & Armament Experimental Establishment (A&AEE) on 27 November 1936; the aircraft was lost on 19 April 1937, after elevators broke off and it crashed near Brightwell, Suffolk. One killed.

- 175 ordered to specification B.29/36 on 15 August 1936; Wellington Mk I (Type 285) as L4212–4311 and L4317–4391 under contract 549268/36 by Vickers, Weybridge. Delivered between July 1938 and August 1939. L4212 built as Type 285 with Pegasus X engines later converted to Type 290 with Pegasus XVIII engines; remainder built as Type 290. L4250 converted to Type 298, Mk II prototype (interim Type 298); L4251 converted to Type 299, Mk III prototype (interim); L4311, 4330, 4340, 4350, 4355 and 4360 originally ordered for Royal New Zealand Air Force (RNZAF) as Type 403 and NZ300–305 but not delivered; L4212, 4221, 4227, 4356 and 4358 converted to directional wireless installation (DWI).

- 20 Mk Is (Type 290/403) and Mk IA (Type 408/412) were ordered as L7770–7789 (L7773 was the only Mk IA from this batch and L7776 was later converted to C Mk XV) under contract 692236/37 by Vickers, Chester. Delivered between August 1939 and April 1940; this contract was originally intended for Gloster.

- 80 Mk ICs (Type 415) were ordered as L7790–7899 under contract 692236/37 by Vickers, Chester. Delivered between April and July 1940. The majority of this batch was delivered direct to Maintenance Units (MU) for modification and later delivery to operational squadrons.

- 100 Mk ICs were ordered as N2735–2784, 2800–2829 and 2840–2859 under contract 692236/27 by Vickers, Chester. Delivered between 2 July and 22 August 1940. All were delivered to MUs; N2755, 2801, 2856 and 2857 were later converted to Mk XVI.

- 120 Mk IAs were ordered as N2865–2914, 2935–2964 and 2980–3019 under contract 549268/36 by Vickers, Weybridge. Delivered between August and 27 December 1939. Twelve from this batch were originally allocated to the RNZAF as NZ306–317, but not delivered. N2867, 2871, 2875, 2877, 2880, 2886, 2887, 2909, 2944, 2947, 2954, 2955 and 2958 were all converted to Mk XV.

- 18 Mk IAs were ordered as P2515–2532 under contract 781439/36 by Vickers, Weybridge. Delivered between December 1938 and January 1940 to replace RNZAF aircraft. P2516 was a prototype DWI conversion; P2518, 2521 and 2522 as Type 418.

- 32 Mk IAs were ordered as P9205–9236 under contract 549268/36 by Vickers, Weybridge. Delivered on 8 January and 11 April 1940. P9238 was converted to Mk III

- 50 Mk ICs were ordered as P9237–9250 and 9265–9300 under contract 549268/36 by Vickers, Weybridge. Delivered between March and April 1940. P9289 was converted to Mk XVI.

- 550 Mk ICs were ordered as R1000–1049, 1060–1099, 1135–1184, 1210–1254, 1265–1299, 1320–1349, 1354–1414, 1435–1474, 1490–1539, 1585–1629, 1640–1669, 1695–1729 and 1757–1806 under contract 992424/39 by Vickers, Chester. Delivered between 22 August 1940 and June 1941. The following 25 aircraft were converted to Mk IV, R1220 (Type 410 prototype), 1390, 1490, 1510, 1515, 1520, 1525, 1530, 1535, 1585, 1590, 1610, 1615, 1620, 1625, 1650, 1655, 1695, 1705, 1715, 1725, 1765, 1775, 1785 and 1795. R1032, 1144, 1172, 1409, 1452, 1521, 1531, 1600, 1605, 1659, 1668, 1700, 1710, 1711 and 1720 were converted to Mk XVI.

- 100 Mk ICs were ordered as R3150–3179, 3195–3239 and 3275–3299 under contract B3913/39 by Vickers, Weybridge. Delivered between 12 April and 9 June 1940. R3221 was converted to Mk II on the production line, and R3298 and R3299 were converted to Mk V. R3217, 3225, 3234 and 3237 were later converted to Mk XVI.

- 300 Mk ICs were ordered as T2458–2477, 2501–2520, 2541–2580, 2606–2625, 2701–2750, 2801–2850, 2873–2922 and 2951–3000 under contract B38600/39 by Vickers, Weybridge. Delivered between 10 June 1940 and 7 February 1941. In total, 293 of this batch were built as Mk IC. Of the remainder, T2545 was built as a Mk II and T2919, 2977, 2979, 2982, 2988 and 2998 were built as Mk VIII. T2850, 2920 and 2969 were later converted to Mk XVI.

- 200 Mk IIs (Type 417) were ordered as W5352–5401, 5414–5463, 5476–5500, 5513–5537, 5550–5598 and 5611 under contract B.71441/40 by Vickers, Weybridge. Delivered between 7 October 1940 and July 1941. W5352 was built as Mk IC, and W5389/G with Merlin 60 engine and wings from Mk VI fitted with Rover-Whittle W2B jet in tail in place of tail turret; maximum altitude reached was 33,000ft.

- 100 Mk ICs were ordered as W5612–5631, 5644–5690 and 5703–5735 under contract B.71441/40 by Vickers, Weybridge. Delivered between February and 4 May 1941. W5615, 5619, 5623, 5631, 5645, 5647, 5649, 5651, 5653, 5655, 5657, 5659, 5661–5662, 5671–5672, 5674, 5676, 5678, 5725, 5628 and 5730–5735 were built as Mk VIII. W5352–5611 were built as Mk II, and W5686 and 5709 were later converted to Mk XVI. W5518/G was fitted W2/700 jet in tail; maximum altitude reached 36,000ft.

- 21 Mk Vs (Type 426) and Mk VIs (Type 431) were ordered as W5795–5815 (W5816–5824 cancelled) under contract 67578/40 by Vickers, Weybridge. Delivered between January and June 1942. Only W5796 was built as a Mk V.

- 50 Mk ICs were ordered as X3160–3179 and 3192–3221 under contract B.92439/40 by Vickers, Squires Gate (Blackpool). Delivered between August 1940 and June 1941. X3193 was converted to Mk XVI.

- 450 Mk IIIs (Type 417) were ordered as X3222–3226, 3275–3289, 3304–3313, 3330–3374, 3387–3426, 3445–3489, 3538–3567, 3584–3608, 3633–3677, 3694–3728, 3741–3754, 3784–3823, 3855–3890, 3923–3957 and 3984–4003 under contract B.92439/40 by Vickers, Squires Gate. Delivered between May 1941 and 6 July 1942. X3374 and X3595 were converted to Mk X, and X3935 was converted to Mk XVI

- 378 Mk ICs were ordered as X9600–9644, 9658–9707, 9733–9757, 9784–9834, 9871–9890, 9905–9954, 9974–9993, Z1040–1054, 1066–1115 and 1139–1181 under contract B97887/39 by Vickers, Hawarden. Delivered between 10 May 1941 and 9 March 1942. X9663, 9678, Z1071 and 1150 were converted to Mk XVI.

- 195 Mk IVs were ordered as Z1182–1183, 1202–1221, 1243–1292, 1311–1345, 1375–1424 and 1459–1496 under contract B97887/40 by Vickers, Hawarden. Delivered between June 1941 and March 1942.

- 137 Mk IIIs were ordered as Z1562–1578, 1592–1626, 1648–1697 and 1717–1751 under contract B97887/40 by Vickers, Hawarden. Delivered between November 1941 and May 1943.

- 200 Mk IIs were ordered as Z8328–8377, 8397–8441, 8489–8538, 8567–8601 and 8643–8662 under contract B71441/40 by Vickers, Weybridge. Delivered between 14 July 1941 and 30 June 1942. Z8416/G was fitted with a 40mm 'S' gun, and Z8570/G had a British Thomson-Houston W2B jet installed in the tail.

- 250 Mk ICs were ordered as Z8702–8736, 8761–8810, 8827–8871, 8891–8910, 8942–8991, 9016–9045 and 9095–9114 under contract B711441/40 by Vickers, Weybridge. Delivered between 7 May and 30 November 1941. The following were converted to Mk VIII; Z8702–8703, 8705–8708, 8710, 8712–8713, 8715, 8717, 8719, 8721, 8723, 8725, 8727, 8892, 8895, 8898, 8902 and 8906. Z8709, 8831 and 8850 were converted to Mk XVI.

- 50 Mk ICs were ordered as AD589–608 and AD624–653 under contract B7144/40 by Vickers, Weybridge. Delivered between 6 December 1941 and 5 January 1942. AD646 became the torpedo-bomber prototype.
- 50 Mk ICs and VIIIs (Type 429) were ordered as BB455–484 and 497–516 by Vickers, Weybridge. Delivered between 6 January and 11 February 1942. The original order was for 150 aircraft. Only seven of this batch were built as Mk VIII, these were BB461, 466, 571, 476, 481, 503 and 513.
- 600 Mk IIIs were ordered as BJ581–625, 642–675, 688–730, 753–801, 818–847, 876–922, 958–991, BK123–166, 179–214, 234–281, 295–315, 330–358, 385–408, 425–471, 489–517 and 534–564 by Vickers, Chester. Delivered between 30 May and 2 December 1942.
- 150 Mk IIIs were ordered as DF542–579, 594–642, 664–709 and 727–743 under contract B92439/40/C.4(c) by Vickers, Blackpool. Delivered between 5 August and 25 September 1942. This order was originally for 400 aircraft. Five aircraft were built as Mk X, serialled DF609, 686, 701, 730 and 740.
- 44 Mk VIs (Type 431), VIAs and VIGs (Type 449) were ordered as DR471–504/G and 519–528/G by Vickers, Weybridge. Delivered between 27 May 1942 and 31 March 1943. DR471–479 were delivered as Mk VIA (Type 442), and DR480–504 and 519–528 as Mk VIG (Type 449).
- 425 Mk ICs were ordered as DV411–458, 473–522, 536–579, 593–624, 638–678, 694–740, 757–786, 799–846, 864–898 and 914–953 under contract 124362/40 by Vickers, Chester. Delivered between 11 November 1941 and 13 June 1942. DV491, 594, 617, 704, 738, 761, 762, 822, 886, 920, 921, 924 and 942 were converted to Mk XVI.
- 15 Mk ICs and one Mk VIII (ES986) were ordered as ES980–995 by Vickers, Weybridge. Delivered between 10 and 19 February 1942. ES986 was converted with a Leigh Light.
- 85 Mk ICs were ordered as HD942–991, HE101–134 and HE146 under contract 124362/40/C4(c) by Vickers, Hawarden. Delivered between June and September 1942.
- 672 Mk Xs (Type 440) were ordered as HE147–184, 197–244, 258–306, 318–353, 365–398, 410–447, 459–508, 513–556, 568–615, 627–667, 679–715, 727–772, 784–833, 845–873, 898–931 and 946–995 under contract 124362/40/C4(c) by Vickers, Hawarden. Delivered between November 1942 and May 1943.
- 251 Mk III (HF112), Mk XII (Type 455) (HF113–120) and Mk XIV (Type 467) (HF121–155, 167–208, 220–252, 264–312, 329–363, 381–422 and 446–451) by Vickers, Squires Gate. Delivered between December 1942 and March 1943.
- 118 Mk Xs ordered as HF452–495, 513–545, 567–606 under contract 124362/40/C4(c) by Vickers, Hawarden. Delivered between May and June 1943.
- 153 Mk III, Mk X and Mk XI (Type 458) ordered as HF609–650, 666–703, 718–764 and 791–816 under contract B.92439/40/C.4(c) by Vickers, Squires Gate. Delivered between 25 September 1942 and 3 February 1943. HF614, 622, 626, 630, 634, 638, 642, 646, 650, 669, 723, 725, 729, 732, 735, 739, 743, 747, 751, 755, 759, 763, 793, 797, 805, 808 and 811 were built as Mk X, HF720 and HF803–804 as Mk XI while the remainder were Mk IIIs.
- 84 Mk ICs and Mk VIIIs were ordered as HF828–869 and 881–922 under contract B.71441/40 by Vickers, Weybridge. Delivered between 19 February and 11 April 1942. HF828, 838, 850, 854, 857, 860, 863, 866, 869, 883, 886, 889, 892, 895, 901, 904, 907, 910, 913, 916, 919 and 922 were built as Mk VIIIs.
- 300 Mk ICs and Mk VIIIs were ordered as HX364–403, 417–452, 466–489, 504–538, 558–606, 625–656, 670–690, 709–751 and 767–786 under contract B.71441/40 by Vickers, Weybridge. Delivered between 12 April and 18 September 1942. The following aircraft were built as Mk IC; HX364–371, 373–375, 377–378, 380, 382, 384-385, 387, 389–390,392–393, 395, 397, 399–400, 402,

417, 421, 423, 425, 429, 431, 433, 435, 438, 440, 442, 445-447, 449, 451, 468, 470, 472, 475, 478, 480, 483–484, 486, 488, 506, 508, 510, 514, 516, 518, 521, 523, 525, 527, 529, 533, 536, 558, 560, 564, 567, 569, 571, 573, 577, 580, 583, 585, 589, 591, 594, 597, 601, 603, 606, 627, 631, 633, 635, 637, 639, 643, 645, 648, 651, 655, 670, 673, 676, 680, 682, 685, 688, 710, 712, 714, 716, 718, 722, 724, 727, 730, 734, 736, 739, 742, 746, 748, 750, 767, 769, 773, 775, 778, 781 and 785.

- 850 Mk IIIs, Mk Xs, Mk XIs (Type 458) and Mk XIIIs were ordered as HZ102–150, 173–209, 242–284, 299–315, 351–378, 394–439, 467–187, 513–554, 570–604, 633–660, 689–727, 752–770, 793–820, 862–897, 937–981, JA104–151, 176–210, 256–273, 295–318, 337–363, 378–426, 442–481, 497–539, 561–585 and 618–645 under contract B.92439/40/C.4(c) by Vickers, Blackpool. Delivered between 20 December 1942 and 20 December 1943. HZ103–104, 106–107, 109–110, 112–113, 115–116, 118–119, 121–122, 124–125, 127–128, 130–131, 133–134, 136–137, 139–140, 145–156, 148–150, 173–174, 176–177, 179–180, 182–183, 185–186, 188–189, 191–192, 194–195, 197–198, 200–201, 203–204, 206–207, 209, 242, 244–245, 247–248, 250 were built as Mk IIIs. The Mk Xs were HZ102, 105, 108, 111, 114, 117, 120, 123, 125, 129, 132, 135, 138, 141, 144, 147, 175, 181, 187, 193, 199, 205, 243, 249, 255–273, 277–282, 300–305, 309–314, 353–358, 362–367, 371–376, 398–403, 410–415, 422–427, 434–439, 457–487, 513–521, 528–533, 540–545, 552–554, 570–572, 579–582, 713–720, 809–818, 941–950, JA111–140, 185–194, 341–352, 448–481, 497–512 and 519–534. Mk XIs were HZ142–143, 178, 184, 190, 196, 202, 208, 246, 251–254, 274–276, 283–284, 299, 306–308, 315, 351–352, 359–351, 368–370, 377–378, 394–397, 404–409, 416–421, 428–433, 522–527, 534–539 and 546–550. Mk XIIIs were HZ551, 573–578, 583–604, 633–660, 689–712, 721–727, 752–770, 793–808, 819–820, 862–897, 937–940, 951–981, JA104–110, 141–151, 176–184, 195–210, 256–318, 337–340, 353–363, 378–426, 442–447, 513–518, 525–539, 561–585 and 618–645.

- 150 Mk ICs and Mk VIIIs were ordered as LA964–998, LB110–156, 169–197 and 213–251 under contract B.71441/40 by Vickers, Weybridge. Delivered between 19 September and 31 October 1942. Another 16 Mk ICs were built serialled LA965, 968, 973, 978, 984, 988, 994, LB110, 116, 120, 126, 131, 141, 148, 152 and 174. The remainder were Mk VIIIs, built as torpedo-bombers or with Leigh Lights.

- 1,382 Mk Xs were ordered as LN157–189, 221–248, 261–303, 317–353, 369–509, 423–458, 481–516, 529–571, 583–622, 633–676, 689–723, 736–778, 791–823, 836–879, 893–936, 948–989, LP113–156, 169–213, 226–268, 281–314, 328–369, 381–415, 428–469, 483–526, 539–581, 595–628, 640–686, 699–733, 748–788, 802–849, 863–889, 901–930, 943–986, LR110–142, 156–164, 168–183 and 195–210 under contract 124362/40/C4(c) with Bristol Hercules XVI engines by Vickers, Hawarden. Delivered between 15 September 1943 and 18 January 1945.

- 600 Mk Xs, Mk XIIIs and Mk XIVs (Type 467) were ordered on 28 May 1942 as ME870–914, 926–960, 972–999; MF113–156, 170–213, 226–267, 279–320, 335–377, 389–424, 439–480, 493–538, 550–596, 614–659, 672–713 and 725–742 under contract B.92439/40/C.4(c) with Hercules XVI engines by Vickers, Squires Gate. Delivered between 10 December 1943 and June 1944. The Mk Xs were serialled ME870–883, 951–960, 972–999; MF113–124, 131–144, 193–202, 236–249, 281–288, 311–316, 346–51, 367–372, 299–304, 421–424, 439–441, 452–459, 468–479, 500–538, 550–572, 583–596, 614–615, 624–635, 644–655, 676–687, 695–706 and 728–739: MF450–451, 726–727 were Mk XIVs; the remainder were Mk XIIIs.

- 250 Mk XIs, Mk XIIs, Mk XIIIs and Mk XIVs were ordered as MP502–549, 562, 601, 615–656, 679–724, 738–774 and 789–825 under contract AIR/2312 by Vickers, Weybridge. Delivered between 5 December 1942 and 18 September 1943. The Mk XIs were MP502, 504, 516–535, 543–549, 562–574, 576–577, 579–580, 582–583, 585–586, 588–589, 591–592, 594–595, 597–598,

Record-breaking Wellington production in full swing at Chester (Hawarden/Broughton), which peaked at 130 aircraft per month in 1942. The Chester plant churned out 5,540 of the 11,461 Wellingtons built. (*Aeroplane*)

600–601, 616–617, 619, 621, 623, 625, 627, 629, 631, 633, 635, 637, 639, 649, 651, 653, 655, 679, 681, 683, 685, 687, 689, 691-703. The Mk XIIs were MP503, 505–515, 536–542, 575, 578, 581, 584, 587, 590, 593, 596, 599, 615, 618,620, 622, 624, 626, 628, 630, 632, 634, 636, 638, 650, 652, 654, 656, 680, 682, 684, 686, 688, 690: Mk XIIs were MP704–709, 711, 713, 715, 717, 719, 721, 723, 738, 740, 742–749, 751, 753, 755, 757, 759, 761–762, 764–765, 767–768, 770–771, 773, 790, 793, 796, 800, 804. The Mk XIVs were MP710, 712, 714, 716, 718, 720, 722, 724, 739, 741, 750, 752, 754, 756, 758, 760, 763, 766, 769, 772, 774, 789, 791–792, 794–795, 797–799, 801–803 and 805–825. MP518, 520, 522, 526, 529, 531–533, 548 later converted to Mk XVII.

- 27 Mk Xs ordered as MS470–496 under contract B.92439/40/C.4(c) by Vickers, Blackpool. Delivered between 3 February and 4 April 1943.
- 263 Mk Xs ordered as NA710–754, 766–811, 823–870, 893–937, 949–997 and NB110–139 under contract B.124362/40 by Vickers, Chester. Delivered between 2 August 1944 and 5 July 1945.
- 296 Mk XIIIs and Mk XIVs ordered as NB767–787, 796–841, 853–896, 908–952, 964–999; NC112–160, 164–209 and 222–234 under contract B.124362/40/C.4(c) by Vickers, Hawarden. Delivered between April and December 1944. Only NB767–771 were built as Mk XIV.
- 500 Mk Xs, Mk XIIIs and Mk XIVs were ordered as NC414–459, 471–517, 529–576, 588–632, 644–692, 706–750, 766–813, 825–870, 883–929, 942–990 and ND104–133 under contract B.92439/40/C.4(c) by Vickers, Squires Gate. Delivered between June and 10 November 1944. The Mk XIIIs were NC414–418, 433, 440, 453–459, 471, 482–489, 503, 510, 534–541, 555–562, 571–576, 588–589, 602–609, 626–631, 656–663 and 741–747. The Mk XIVs were NC419–420, 441–442, 490–493, 511–513, 542–544, 490–591, 610–613, 622–625, 632, 644–647, 672–677, 771–776, 785–788, 797–800, 828–835, 848–855, 870, 883–889, 902–907 and ND129–133. NC868–869, 926–928 and ND104–128 were converted to Mk XVIII.
- 400 Mk Xs, Mk XIVs and Mk XVIIIs (Type 490) were ordered as PF820–866, 879–915, 927–968, 979–999, PG112–157, 170–215, 227–269, 282–326, 338–379 and 392–422 under contract B.92439/40/C.4(c) by Vickers, Blackpool. Delivered between November 1944 and April 1945. Mk XIVs were PF820–822, 831–838, 847–854, 863–866, 879–882, 889–893, 902–911, 931–940, 949–958, 967–968, 979–986, 995–999, PG112–116, 125–134, 139–148, 153–157, 170–174, 183–192, 197–206, 211–215, 227–231, 240–245, 266–269, 282–285 and 298–303. Mk XVIIIs were PG236–239, 246–249, 254–257, 349, 356, 367–370 and 395–400.
- 226 Mk Xs and Mk XVIIIs were ordered as RP312–358, 373–415, 428–469, 483–526, 538–561 and 565–590 under contract B.92439/40/C.4(c) by Vickers, Blackpool. Delivered between 7 May and 25 October 1945. RP330–335, 348–351, 392–395, 412–415, 428–429 were built as Mk XVIII.

Chapter 4

All Commands Across the Globe

It was an unfortunate coincidence that the specification for Britain's latest heavy aircraft was issued in 1932, at the same time as the Geneva Conference on Disarmament was calling for a cap of 6,500lb on all bombers. If carried through, this restriction would have eliminated the sight of all 'heavy' bombers across Europe, leaving the RAF only capable of carrying a small bomb load as far as the English Channel or the North Sea. History would show that a certain country in Western Europe would completely disregard this criteria and Britain would respond with aircraft of increasing weight and capability. Crucially, it would be designs that were presented by Vickers and Handley Page to Specification B.9/32, which would evolve into the Wellington and the Hampden, both aircraft proving vital to early Bomber Command operations, alongside the Blenheim and the Whitley.

Into service

The first Wellington Mk Is, in place of the Handley Page Heyford, joined 99 Sqn at Mildenhall under the command of Wg Cdr HE Walker MC in October 1938. 38 Sqn at Marham, under the command of Wg Cdr ES Goodwin DFC, re-equipped in November, the unit not shedding a tear as their Fairey Hendons were flown away. By the beginning of World War Two the RAF had ten Wellington squadrons, all part of 3 Group, based in East Anglia under the command of Air Vice-Marshal JEA Baldwin CB, DSO, OBE who had his HQ at Mildenhall.

Crews of 149 Squadron walk out to their Wellingtons at Mildenhall in late 1939. 149 Squadron and 9 Squadron bore the brunt of the Wimpys' early daylight operations.

Throughout the summer of 1939, 3 Group had taken part in many exercises in Britain and France, the latter intending to demonstrate to Germany that Britain was ready. The training and the exercises that the Wellington crews were involved in were all carried out in daylight. It was thought that this new generation of bomber could easily defend itself thanks to its turreted armament, and attack military and industrial targets at will, deep into Germany. As a result, when war was declared, none of the RAF Wellington squadrons were operational at night and, as time would tell, when they did begin nocturnal duties, the primitive equipment and methods, specifically navigation and bomb-aiming, were not up to the job.

Early action

On 3 September 1939, both the Wellington and Hampden were in the air and on the hunt for enemy shipping but none were forthcoming. The following day, the Wellington was in action for the first time, when 9 and 149 Squadrons were despatched to bomb German warships at Brunsbüttel. It was an inauspicious start; of the 14 aircraft that were sent, only four crews managed to bomb on target because of a navigational error, which also resulted in two bombs being dropped on the Danish town of Esbjerg, 100 miles north of Brunsbüttel! Two bombers, L4275 and L4292, failed to return.

Squadrons from Stradishall, West Suffolk, show off their new early production Wellington Mk Is in the spring 1939. The unit went on to operate the Mk IA, IC (twice!), II and III, before re-equipping with the Lancaster Mk I and III in September 1942.

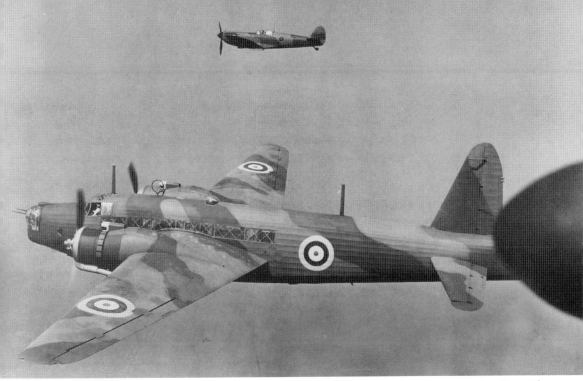

A scene that was sadly not repeated during the Wellington's early daylight operations because neither the Spitfire, nor any other RAF fighter at the time, possessed the range to escort a bomber to German targets.

The Fraser-Nash FN.5 front turret was a marked improvement over the original Vickers turret, installed into the early production aircraft. Each .303in Browning machine gun was supplied with 1,000 rounds of ammunition with a 1,000-round reserve for each gun stored in the fuselage. (Via *Aeroplane*)

The defensive armament of the early production Wellingtons was under scrutiny from the outset. The retractable ventral 'dustbin' was particularly unpopular with the crews and the forward and rear turrets were only classed as rudimentary by senior staff. 3 Group had complained that the bomber's turrets were woefully inadequate against a determined fighter attack but this did not stop 214 and 215 Squadrons, stationed at Methwold (Norfolk) and Bassingbourn (Cambridgeshire) respectively, from re-equipping with these early Wellingtons.

Up to early December 1939, the Wellington was employed on 'North Sea sweep' operations and the bomber enjoyed a period of 55 sorties without loss. In the meantime, the delivery of the Fraser-Nash turreted Wellington Mk IA was given priority in an effort to subdue 3 Group's worries about the type's ability to protect itself. The next major raid that the Wellington took part in was on 3 December, when 24 aircraft of 38, 115 and 149 Squadrons attacked enemy warships at Heligoland. A single hit was claimed on a cruiser and once the local fighters, Bf109s and Bf110s were alerted, one of the former was claimed as shot down without loss to the Wellington force. Bomber Command quickly deduced from this single operation that the bomber was more than capable of protecting itself and could, as planned, penetrate enemy defences in daylight. The first opportunity for the new Mk IA to prove itself came on December 14, when a dozen aircraft from 99 Squadron were ordered to attack a convoy in the Schilling Roads, north of Wilhelmshaven. Heavy cloud forced the bombers down to low level where they were engaged by flak and fighters. Five Wellingtons failed to return, three of them claimed by fighters and two more colliding trying to avoid them, while one enemy fighter was shot down.

The final straw came on December 18, in an action that would shape the future of Bomber Command tactics for the remainder of the war. Still adamant that heavy bombers could look after themselves in broad daylight without a fighter escort, 24 Wellingtons from 9, 37 and 149 Squadrons were despatched again to attack warships off Wilhelmshaven. Ordered to attack above 10,000ft to avoid the worst of the flak, 22 aircraft bombed in crystal clear conditions from 13,000ft, while the defending fighters were directed by a ground controller, for the first time, towards their quarry. Already aware that the Wellington could not protect itself from a high beam attack because the front and rear guns could not traverse through 180 degrees, the onslaught began. In a short space of time, the pilots of II/Jg2 shot down nine Wellingtons and three more were forced into the sea because they were so badly damaged. Two German fighters were shot down but, as with the earlier raids, no bombs fell on the intended target.

A change of policy

In the space of a few days, nearly 100 Wellington aircrew were dead, wounded or missing and out of the 36 aircraft despatched, 21 had been lost with nothing to show for their sacrifice. This loss rate was clearly unsustainable and the senior Air Staff finally conceded that daylight operations in the enemy's own back yard were not the way forward for Bomber Command's 'heavy' bombers. Battles and Blenheims would continue to fight it out until the end of the Battle of France but future daylight operations would only be carried out with a substantial fighter escort and, even then, the odds of success for the bomber were low, until aerial superiority was gained.

From early 1940, the Wellington joined the Whitley on night operations, although until April, these only entailed leaflet-dropping sorties, known as Nickels, over Germany. The loss rate dramatically reduced for the Wellington when it went nocturnal, but the accuracy in navigation and bomb aiming also dropped and it was not unusual for the target to be missed by many miles during these early forays.

Once restrictions were lifted with regard to total aerial warfare, the Wellington quickly settled in to night operations and, at the time, was the only serious contender for taking the fight directly back to the German homeland. Strategic bombing of Germany began following the evacuation of Dunkirk as well as a few targets in Italy. From June, the Wellington was involved in the destruction of the many invasion

The FN.5 rear turret of a Wellington Mk IC; the lonely domain of 'tail-end Charlie', and when approached from below, was one of the most vulnerable points of the aircraft, which early enemy fighter tactics fully exploited.

barges, which were gathering in Channel ports during the Battle of Britain.

By the time Air Marshal Sir Richard Peirse took over as Air Officer Commanding (AOC), Bomber Command, from Air Marshal Sir Charles Portal in October 1940, 100 Wellingtons were on charge out of a total strength of 230 aircraft. The bomber stream was yet to be invented during this period and it was not unusual for single aircraft to be despatched to a single target. Interceptions by enemy fighters suddenly became very rare during these early night operations and the Wellington began a period of popularity with its crews. Reliable and incredibly strong even when it suffered the most appalling flak damage, the Wellington quickly built the reputation of an aircraft that would always get you home.

Improving effectiveness

The Wellington Mk IA was at the limit of its capability when carrying a full bomb load, but the arrival of the much improved Mk IC, took the aircraft to a new level. First was the armament issue, which saw the removal of dustbin turret, replaced by a pair of manually-traversing .303in on each side of the fuselage. The bomb bay was modified so that it could carry a pair of 2,000lb AP and two 250lb GP bombs, which was the standard load carried on operations up to 1,500 miles. The Merlin-powered Mk II joined 12 Squadron in October 1940 and 142 Squadron in November, both of which were glad to see the back of their Battles and were both stationed at Binbrook. The Mk II was capable of carrying one of Bomber Command's most successful pieces of ordnance, the 4,000lb 'Cookie', the largest single weapon carried by a British bomber to date when it was first employed in March 1941. The device entered service when a Wellington from 9 Squadron and from 149 Squadron dropped the parachute bomb over Emden on 31 March /1 April 1941.

The Hercules-powered Mk III was the next Wimpy to enter service; a variant that would prove particularly useful in the Middle East, thanks to tropicalisation, additional long-range fuel tanks and mounts for air filters. Demand for the Pegasus, Hercules and Merlin engines saw the introduction of the Pratt & Whitney Twin Wasp-powered Mk IV. The majority of the 220 built served with Polish units, including 300, 301 and 305 Squadrons.

Back in August 1940, the Air Staff announced that the future of Bomber Command would be dominated by four-engined types, beginning with the Halifax and Stirling, which entered service in November 1940 and January 1941 respectively. It would be another three years before this was realised as the Wellington continued to remain in the front line and was only half through its production life when the Mk X was introduced in late 1942.

By November 1941, Wellingtons formed more than 40 per cent of Bomber Command's strength, peaking in January 1942 when 25 operational squadrons were equipped with the twin-engined bomber. When Peirse was dismissed in February 1942, his successor, Air Chief Marshal Sir Arthur Harris, was very keen to demonstrate how powerful Bomber Command was by organising three 'thousand bomber' raids. Of the 1,047 aircraft that took part in the first raid on Cologne on 30–31 May, 602 of them were Wellingtons, although 303 of these were supplied from the OTUs. Wellingtons also played a major role in the next two 'thousand bomber' raids against Essen on 1–2 June (545 Wellingtons out of a total of 956 aircraft), and Bremen on 25–26 June (474 Wellingtons out of a total of 960 aircraft).

Harris was also instrumental in accelerating the production of the four-engined heavies, which by then, also included the Lancaster, which had entered service in December 1941. While the Hampden, Whitley and eventually the Blenheim were removed from the fight over Europe, the Wellington continued on much longer. The final raid that Bomber Command Wellingtons participated in was to Hannover on 8–9 October 1943, when 300 and 432 Squadrons contributed 26 aircraft, which all returned safely. The type never fully faded out Bomber Command duties though, as Wellingtons were employed by OTUs on Nickels. Mine-laying continued and the type also operated in the Electronic Intelligence (ELINT) role until the end of war.

The Middle East and Mediterranean

The RAF was well represented in the Middle East when war broke with regard to numbers of aircraft. However, the 20 squadrons on strength were all operating obsolete aircraft, including the bomber units

While one airman forces a grin as he lifts himself through the forward ventral entry hatch, the rest of the crew concentrate on tending to their kit, seemingly oblivious to the photographer.

whose most effective aircraft was another geodetic creation, the Wellesley. Wellingtons first arrived in the theatre in the shape of the special-duty Directional Wireless Installation (DWI) from May 1940. 70 Squadron at Kabrit was the first unit to receive the Wellington Mk I in September 1940, in place of the Valentia. These aircraft were quickly pressed into service on raids against Benghazi.

Three units, 37, 28 and 148 Squadrons, were posted to the Middle East to bolster the low-priority theatre, the aircraft engaging in raids on Italy and Western Libya en route from Malta. The Wellingtons played an important role in Operation *Compass* supporting British forces when they pushed westwards from Egypt into Libya. Several Wellingtons also served in Greece following the Italian invasion but were forced to withdraw when the German forces pushed harder than their allies.

As with all units during the North African campaign, the Wellington squadrons were continually on the move as the battle pushed back and forth, unlike their cousins back in England who were operating from a single, comparatively comfortable, well-equipped airfield. Spares were in short supply, the conditions were brutal but the hard-working RAF 'erks' kept the Wimpys flying.

The DWI aircraft, which were mainly used in the Mediterranean theatre, was first conceived in January 1940 when several Mk Is were converted to explode German magnetic sea mines. To do this, a 48ft diameter hoop was attached to the nose, underside of the wings and the rear fuselage. The hoop contained a giant magnetic coil, which was powered by a Ford V8 engine that drove a 35kW Maudsley generator from inside the fuselage. A more powerful de Havilland Gipsy engine was installed in later aircraft, which between January 1940 and early 1944, destroyed 39 mines.

Another role in which the Wellington is rarely recognised is that of the torpedo bomber, a story that began in 1941 when the Royal Navy's Fleet Torpedo Office, Cdr Watson, went searching for an aircraft to deal with Rommel's supply convoys. 38 Squadron at Shallufa was approached and made available one of its precious bombers for conversion to carry a pair of Mk XII torpedoes in the outer bomb cells. Flight

301 (Pomeranian) Squadron, one of several Polish units was formed at Bramcote, Nottinghamshire, in July 1940 with the Fairey Battle. After moving to Swinderby, Lincolnshire, where this atmospheric image was taken, the squadron re-equipped with the Wellington Mk IC in October 1940. (Via *Aeroplane*)

One of a batch of 450 Wellington Mk IIIs built by Vickers at Squires Gate, X3763 only served with 425 (Alouette) Squadron at Dishforth, Yorkshire. The bomber was one of 25 aircraft that failed to return from a raid on Stuttgart on 14–15 April 1943. The crew, Plt Off A T Doucette DFC, Royal Canadian Air Force (RCAF), Sgt A Jones, Plt Off J O L Desroches DFC, RCAF, Sgt D Vollans, Plt Off G P H Ledoux RCAF and Flt Sgt P P Trudeau RCAF were all killed when the Wellington crashed at Mussey-sur-Marne (Haute Marne). (*Aeroplane*)

trials began in December 1941 and, after completion, not without incident, 38 Squadron sunk its first ship with a torpedo on 27 March 1942.

With Rommel's defeat in North Africa in early 1943, Wellingtons found themselves continuing bombing operations to Italy from North African and Maltese airfields. With the invasion of Italy, the Wellington continued on the frontline until March 1945, by which time the bulk of bomber squadrons in theatre had re-equipped with the Liberator.

The Far East

It was not until 1942 that the first Wellingtons arrived in the Far East for service with 99 and 215 Squadrons operating from Indian airfields. The first operations, from Pandaveswar, Bengal, began in April, these generally being long-range night missions against Japanese positions in Burma. Operations were challenging for the RAF crews in this region, with high mountain ranges to negotiate, not to mention tropical storms and varying winds, combined with severe icing conditions at altitude compared to the heat and humidity on the ground.

99 and 215 Squadrons were the only Wellington units to operate from India during 1942 and 1943, but in March and June 1943, both relocated to Jessore. In November 1943, both units became part of Air Command Southeast Asia, which also controlled 8 and 244 Squadrons in the Arabian Peninsula, and 203 and 621 Squadrons, which moved from Africa to Santacruz, Bombay and Aden. All four units served out their days in the maritime reconnaissance role equipped with the GR Mk XIII.

99 Squadron, equipped with the Mk X from April 1943, flew its last Wellington raid to Burma in August 1944 when the Liberator took over. 215 Squadron followed a similar path and the unit re-equipped with the Liberator B Mk VI in July 1944.

Statistics

The Wellington achieved some impressive operational statistics during its service with Bomber Command. The bomber flew 47,409 sorties and dropped 42,000 tons of bombs, which was only surpassed by the Halifax (82,773 sorties) and the Lancaster (156,192 sorties) in RAF service. In total, 1,727 aircraft were lost, equating to a loss rate of 3.64 per cent, which puts the Wellington behind the Mosquito (0.78 per cent), Lancaster (2.35 per cent) and Halifax (2.52 per cent). Operational flying hours from British bases reached at least 350,000 hours plus another 175,000 hours amassed from Middle and Far East operations. Training hours, thanks to the Wellington's prolific use by a number of OTUs for the majority of the war, added at least 1 million flying hours and between 1945 and the type's retirement, another 350,000 hours were flown.

One of Britain's great design icons, the Wellington, became an excellent aircraft because it was available when needed and in huge numbers. The bomber's novel geodetic construction, which had already been employed in Barnes Wallis's early airship designs and the Wellesley bomber, did not prove to be as difficult to construct by a semi-skilled labour force as the Wellington's critics had predicted. This was rubber stamped by the fact that more Wimpys were built than any other bomber in British military aircraft manufacturing history and will never be surpassed.

Chapter 5

The Wimpy Goes to Sea

'S alty' Wimpys played a significant part in the eventual defeat of the ocean wolves, destroying, or at least seriously damaging, a minimum of 51 submarines during 1942–45 and doubtless, if unconsciously, preventing or dissuading unknown numbers of possible attacks on merchant shipping convoys merely by their ever-vigilant presence. As with all Coastal Command operations, irrespective of aircraft type, anti-submarine patrol work was an accumulation of endless hours of 'watching water'; monotonous flying, which rarely produced even a sniff of a U-boat, let alone any form of visible success. It was a task requiring stoic patience and physical endurance, combined with a talent for instant reaction on those rare occasions when a submarine was spotted.

One vital ingredient of success was the Leigh Light; a moveable swivelling searchlight remote from the cockpit, usually in a Wellington, in the mid-belly position, for night illumination of any detected, surfaced U-boat. No.1417 Flight RAF was formed at RAF Chivenor, Devon, to develop the Leigh Light Wellington and to form the nucleus of 172 Squadron as the first Leigh Light unit for maritime operations.

Wellington Mk XIV, MP714, presents an intimidating angle, which would not have been appreciated by any U-boat commander. The aircraft trialled the use of eight 60lb rocket projectiles; they were never used operationally. (Via Martyn Chorlton)

Introducing the Leigh Light

Among the first air crews posted in was Donald Fraser, whose account of those embryo days follows:

'I was a Royal Canadian Air Force (RCAF) Warrant Officer 1st Class pilot with 150 Squadron in RAF Bomber Command when I was posted in early February 1942 to 1417 Flight of Coastal Command Development Unit (CCDU). I was not enamoured with the Wellington and was looking forward to a new challenge. My arrival at Chivenor, late Sunday night, 8 February 1942, was not very auspicious. I learned immediately that in the Chivenor Beaufort OTU there had been three fatal crashes during the past two nights. Therefore, I was relieved somewhat when I was told, next morning, that 1417 Flight was not connected with the OTU, but was a 'hush-hush' unit located in a far hangar. Imagine my reaction when I first saw the plane, a white Wellington with porcupine-like vertical and horizontal aerials sticking out of the fuselage, and two forward-pointing Yagi aerials under the wings. There was no nose turret, but the front was covered with Perspex to give a greenhouse appearance, Leigh's invention was ready for practical testing.

'I soon realised that most Coastal Command pilots had trained on other types of aircraft and that the unit was anxious to have somebody with flying experience on Wellingtons. An outline of problems involved in U-boat detection and destruction was presented by the commanding officer, Wg Cdr Jeff Greswell. U-boats in early 1942 were crossing the Bay of Biscay at night with impunity on the surface on their way to their second 'Happy Time' where they could attack undefended shipping off the coast of the USA. Airborne radar (ASV) had already been installed in the Wellington and had permitted homing-in on surfaced U-boats, with a maximum detection range of about seven miles. But frequently, with a sea run-in, in the last mile contact was lost due to sea return on the radar screen. Hence the Leigh Light, which was installed in the mid-under turret position.

'The next four months were devoted to intensive training. The effective operation of the searchlight had to be co-ordinated with its controls mounted in the nose of the aircraft. The light was to be lowered below the fuselage when ASV contact was made, and swung back and forth, up and down, until the object of the ASV blips was detected. The Helwick Light Vessel in the Bristol Channel served for practice detection at night. Practice bombing was done against a floating target off the steep cliffs of North Devon; the aircraft would approach from the land, dive towards the floating target to simulate an attack on a surfaced U-boat from 1,000ft altitude and one mile distance. This training was not without its casualties. One Wellington, with the squadron's gunnery and navigation officers, a Flight commander, and a full crew, homed in on a blip, which they thought was the Helwick Light Vessel. Unfortunately, the blip was an American tanker steaming up the Bristol Channel. Its alert crew opened fire; the burning Wellington fell into the sea. There were no survivors.

More Wimpys needed

'Originally there was only one Wellington with Leigh Light available for training purposes. Greswell sent a signal to Group HQ to "request some operationally-tired Wimpys from Bomber Command to familiarise our pilots flying the Wimpy and to perfect their low-level bombing techniques". Gradually more Leigh Light Wellingtons became available, but slowly, ever so slowly. Their assignment priority seemed obvious; the first to the Wing Commander, the next two to the Flight Commanders, the fourth to Plt Off Blackmore, an experienced CCDU pilot. WO Fraser was, naturally, further down the list. Another Canadian, Plt Off Russ, arrived, and he was assigned to fly as second pilot and searchlight operator with Plt Off Blackmore's crew. Russ was first on a short ferry flight to St Eval in Cornwall. It was a misty day; his plane disappeared. The following week, the wreck was found on the cliffs behind Hartland Point, near Chivenor. I had, by then, my own crew but no aeroplane, so I immediately volunteered to fly with Blackmore in Russ's place until I got my own aircraft.

'Training went on. Sqn Ldr Leigh periodically showed up on the station to oversee developments. The three-tiered bomb bay held the four Torpex-filled depth charges, the long case of batteries for the searchlight, and an overload fuel tank. The Wellington flew tail down even with trim. Blackmore and I worked on an obvious solution, moving the batteries into the nose of the machine. A wooden case for the 14 batteries was built under the searchlight operator's seat in front of the pilot. The aeroplane now flew better. With an all-up weight of 33,000lb, the two 980hp Bristol Pegasus engines were severely tested. Even in Bomber Command, the same aircraft had an all-up weight of only 29,500lb. The unfavourable power/weight ratio affected the single-engine flying characteristics of the aircraft, but this was later rectified when l,425hp Hercules engines replaced the old Pegasus. It had taken four months, perhaps not really very long under the circumstances, but by early June 1942 the Leigh Light Wellingtons were ready to be tested in battle.

Leigh Light becomes operational

'The first operational sorties of 172 Squadron were flown by four aircraft on the night of 3–4 June 1942, and Greswell was the first to draw blood, flying aircraft 'F'. As he homed in on an ASV blip near the coast of Spain, he lowered his searchlight and illuminated a submarine dead ahead. He overshot it because his altimeter had given a wrong altitude, due to changing barometric pressures this many hundreds of miles from base. (It was some months later before a radio-altimeter corrected this problem.) On his second run-in, the submarine fired recognition signals into the air. Was it a British sub? Then Greswell recalled that British submarines never shot up recognition signals, but burned flares on the surface. He attacked, dropping a stick of Torpex depth charges across the submarine's bows.

'The effect of Greswell's attack is best described directly from the log of the Italian submarine, the Luigi Torelli, of the 1,200-ton Marconi class. On the night of 3–4 June 1942, on a true course of 264 degrees and

A Leigh Light-equipped Wellington GR.XIV; the device is just visible in front of the port main wheel, under the fuselage. This variant equipped 11 operational Coastal Command squadrons. (Via Martyn Chorlton)

Named after the Japanese scientist who invented it in the 1930s, this directional Yagi aerial is under the starboard wing of a Wellington Mk VIII. (Via Martyn Chorlton)

at a speed of nine knots, latitude 44 degrees 43' N, longitude 06 degrees 46' W, it was surprised by the first Leigh Light Wellington at 02:27hrs. The captain of the *Luigi Torelli* (Lt Cdr Augusto Migliorini) reported a sudden appearance of a huge searchlight on a low-flying plane. It illuminated an area about 300m to the right of his bow, then centred upon him. Immediately, the navigation officer on duty gave orders to steam full speed ahead and turn to the left. However, the aircraft kept overhead with its light on the submarine. Finally, it was switched off. The night was very dark with no moon, but much phosphorescence on the sea. Now the captain reduced his speed to a minimum, believing that the aeroplane was detecting him by his phosphorescent wake. As he prepared to dive, the searchlight of the aeroplane lit up again his stern from the right side, approximately 300m away, then centred on the conning tower of the submarine. The captain turned to the right and gave orders to open fire with the anti-aircraft guns. The plane passed over him low (250ft height) also firing, then turned off its searchlight again. When the captain thought that the aircraft had lost him because of his small wake he gave orders for a rapid dive.

'But all was not over. While the captain still had his head stuck out of the hatch, the submarine was again illuminated from a very close range. The bosun had signalled with the hooter to dive when the captain gave orders to turn to port. Only seconds later, the ship was bracketed by a stick of 250lb depth charges that exploded under its hull. The *Luigi Torelli*, covered by columns of water, jerked violently and went down by the bow. As a result of the explosion the catch freed itself from the hook and the hatch closed by itself over the captain's head while the diesel motors were still running. This created a very strong decompression before the motor could be stopped. The captain therefore introduced air into the chambers with the watertight doors near the bow to equalise the air pressure. Although out of the immediate line of fire, the *Luigi Torelli's* troubles were still not over. In some three minutes, the conning tower hatch cover opened again and the bosun's mate, who was still outside, told the captain that the aeroplane was still near; it had passed over twice, firing its machine guns.

'The captain's Log gives the damages resulting from Greswell's attack: Breakage of a considerable number of battery elements that resulted in leakage of acid. Fire in the chambers of two batteries, accompanied by smoke in the chambers over the batteries. Complete loss of power. Damage to compass and steering apparatus. Some development of chlorine. Breakage of shelves and fixtures.

He considered the condition of the interior of the *Luigi Torelli* and decided to steer to a French port (St Jean-de-Luz). The battery fire was not extinguished or even diminished, and strong smoke was produced mainly in the wireless cabin and the officers' and NCOs' quarters. Repeated attempts to enter the front chambers with extinguishers failed. The captain ordered flooding of the ammunition store in the bow after retrieval of the cannon shells, and at length the fire was extinguished.

'In the meantime, Greswell and his crew spotted a second submarine nearby. He is now of the opinion that it may have never seen him because it was submerging when spotted with ASV and searchlight. What saved both these submarines was the failure of the pursuer to get a signal of the attack to the other three Wellingtons on patrol in the area, and home them to the place of the attacks. I was second pilot and searchlight operator on the nearest Wellington, and can testify that no message of this attack was received. Undoubtedly the coded signal '472' ("Sighted sub. Am attacking") had been sent to base at Chivenor, though it may not have reached there immediately because of the low level at which the aircraft was flying when the signal was sent or because of atmospheric disruptions. This weakness in communication was later rectified when attacking aircraft remained in the vicinity of the attack as long at their fuel supply would permit in order to home other aircraft into the area.

Nicknamed the 'Stickleback', for obvious reasons, this Wellington Mk VIII, W5674 is carrying the codes of 221 Squadron in July 1941, although the unit was not officially re-equipped with the variant until January 1942. (Via Martyn Chorlton)

WELLINGTON VI
PEGASUS XVIII

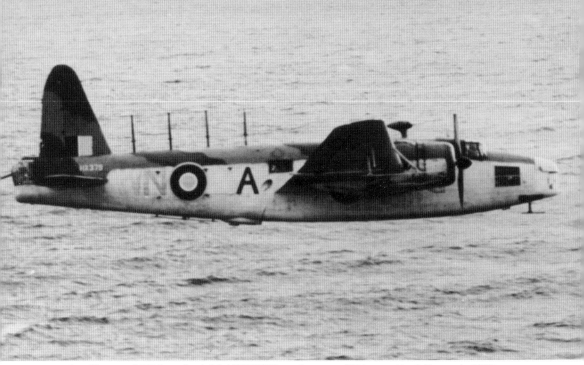

An operational image of 172 Squadron's Mk VIII HX379, on duty out of Chivenor, North Devon, in 1942. 172 Squadron was formed out of 1417 Flight at Chivenor on 2 April 1942. (Via Martyn Chorlton)

38 Squadron operated a variety of Wellington marks from the Mk I in November 1938 through to the GR Mk XIV, which was retired in December 1946. These are GR Mk XIVs operating out of Luqa, Malta, a few weeks after the war ended in Europe. (Via Martyn Chorlton)

'In any case, the *Luigi Torelli* escaped. Other submarines later attacked by Leigh Light-equipped anti-submarine aircraft were not that lucky. Shortly after, my own connection with 172 Squadron ended when, in mid-August, I was commissioned and posted to Wick, where another Leigh Light Wellington squadron, 179, was then forming.'

Wellington Mk XIII, JA205 of 621 Squadron during an operational sortie out of Khormaksar, Yemen, in 1944. (Via Martyn Chorlton)

The lucky *Luigi Torelli*

The *Luigi Torelli* was to have a long and chequered career after this first encounter with 172 Squadron. On 5 June 1942, she was hastily repaired in a Spanish harbour, left this haven on 6 June, only to be attacked twice by Sunderlands of 10 Royal Australian Air Force (RAAF) Squadron and further damaged. Putting in to the Spanish port of Santander, the submarine was officially interned; yet a month later made a dash to freedom. In 1943, it went to the Far East, was taken over by the Germans after Italy's surrender and retitled UIT-25; then when Germany surrendered in May 1945, was retaken-over by the Japanese who titled her RO-504. Four months later, she fell into American hands, but was finally scuttled by her ultimate (sixth) captain in 1946. 172 Squadron's first true kill was to come just four weeks after Greswell's attack, on 6 July 1942, when an American pilot in the unit, Plt Off W. Howell in Wellington 'H' sunk the U-502.

304 Squadron in action

The successes of the Leigh Light Wellingtons were to continue until the final victory in Europe in May 1945; with the final confirmed U-boat sinking by a Wimpy occurring on 2 April 1945 when Wellington 'Y-Yorker' of 304 (Silesian) Squadron sank U-321 at the location 50 degrees N, 12 degrees 57' W. Indeed, as merely one example of the sustained effort made by the maritime Wellington squadrons, the record of 304 Squadron shows that during its three years' sojourn with Coastal Command, its crews had flown 2,451 sorties, accumulating therein 21,331 operational flying hours. During these they attacked 34 U-boats and sighted nine others, had 31 combats with German fighters, and lost 106 aircrew killed or missing. In balance, the Poles of 304 Squadron could claim just two U-boats destroyed and a third seriously damaged. The first confirmed sinking came on 18 June 1944, when Flt Lt J. Antoniewicz, skippering Wellington 'A-Able', destroyed U-441, killing its captain Kapitanleutnant Klaus Hartmann and his entire crew.

U-441 was nearing the end of a two-week patrol and some 50 miles from its intended haven at Brest when it had the misfortune to cross the path of Antoniewicz's Wellington; the aircraft having had a complete breakdown in its radar-search equipment and merely relying on the 'Eyeball Mk 1' for the completion of its patrol in the bright moonlight. What followed was contained in the prosaic terms of the Wellington skipper's official report of 20 June:

'Wellington A/304 on A-U patrol "V" was flying on course 324 degrees(T) when at 22:54hrs (June 18) Captain sighted 050 degrees, red, four miles, a thin trail of vaporous grey smoke on the sea. Weather was fine, visibility four–five miles, sea calm, 9/10ths cloud at 2,000ft. Captain was just about to alter course to investigate when he sighted 045 degrees, green, three miles, black object, which he identified almost immediately as the conning tower of a surfacing U-boat. He turned to port to get on an attacking course. At the same time he lost height. He approached U-boat on a course between 060 and 090(T). When one mile away second pilot and radar operator, in the astrodome, sighted another U-boat which had apparently just surfaced l0 degrees, green, 1½ miles away. Captain kept on his course to attack first U-boat, which then started to submerge slowly. At 22:57hrs six DCs were dropped from 100ft, spaced 60ft, and set to 14–18ft, 155 degrees, green to U-boat heading. Rear gunner distinctly saw positions of entry, the first two hitting the water to starboard quarter of UB (U-boat) (No.2 about 10yds away from hull) and the remainder across the UB and on its port bow. Then he saw them explode, and the explosions and plumes completely obscured UB. He also saw a long black pipe-like object blown about 100ft into the air with the DC explosion. When the explosion plumes subsided there was no sign of the UB, and the conning tower was only just visible when the DCs were dropped. Aircraft then returned to port. Almost immediately after the attack the second UB was seen to submerge. One minute later, the aircraft tracked over the scene of the attack and saw: "(1) Two flame floats burning about 500ft apart. (2) Between the flame floats a spreading bubbling patch of oil. (3) Close to the second flame float two dark cylindrical-looking objects about 30ft long. (4) A considerable quantity of smaller pieces of wreckage between the flame floats."

Regarding the bubbling oil patch, this was first seen by radar operator in the astrodome as soon as DC explosion had subsided. Aircraft made three more runs over the scene, and during the second run (1½ mins after the first) the oil seemed to be gushing to the surface and spreading outwards into a circle fringed with iridescence. At the third run (about 2½ mins after the second) the bubbles and gushing had ceased and the oil patch exceeded in size the area of 500ft between the flame floats. During the fourth run the oil patch was still spreading and the wreckage described above was still evident. Having dropped marine markers, the aircraft then set course on patrol at 23:12hrs.'

'Side-show' successes

If Wellingtons were prominent in the unending campaign against the U-boat in European and Atlantic waters, they were not the only active or successful Wimpys in this role. One example of Wimpy labours in the 'side-show' zones of operations was 621 Squadron. Formed initially at Port Reitz, Kenya, in September 1943 and equipped with Wellingtons for general reconnaissance of the approaches to the Red Sea et al, 621 was based at Aden by early 1944 with various detachments in the area. Their operational area was vast, including the Persian Gulf, while enemy activity was by no means minimal; in January 1944 alone, 16 sightings of U-boats were reported.

On the morning of 2 May 1944, Wellington 'T-Tommy' of 621 Squadron was carrying out an anti-submarine patrol just south of the Gulf of Aden. Skippered by Flt Lt R. H. Mitchell, its other crew members were WO Harvey Riddell, the Canadian second pilot, Flt Sgt O. Gomersal, Navigator and two W/Op AGs, Sgts W. R. Stevenson and S. Philips. They could hardly believe their eyes when they suddenly came upon a U-boat, fully surfaced and steaming along at about 12 knots. Swinging immediately into an attack run, Mitchell bore in for the kill. The U-boat was U-852, commanded by Heinz Eck, which had been active in the area for several weeks, and on spotting the incoming Wimpy, Eck gave immediate

Wimpy aircrew preparing to drop a flame float during an operation over the North Sea. (Crown Copyright via Martyn Chorlton)

orders for a crash-dive – too late. At 800yds range, the Wellington's front guns opened up, slashing a hail of bullets round the conning tower, and at 50ft a stick of six depth charges was placed with deadly accuracy up-track, two of these at least falling within lethal range of the sub's hull. The damage caused was severe enough to prevent the U-boat submerging and she wallowed helplessly on the surface.

Signals were sent from Wimpy 'T-Tommy' for assistance in finally 'nailing' the sitting duck and six further attacks by aircraft from 621 and 8 Squadrons were made during daylight hours; each attack being fiercely contested by the crippled U-boat's gunners. Meanwhile, HMS Falmouth, at the time of 'T-Tommy's' initial attack escorting a convoy from Mombasa to Aden, was ordered to leave the convoy and proceed to the scene. Early next morning, the U-boat was sighted and before Falmouth could reach her, Eck ordered the submarine to be scuttled and set on fire, while surviving crew members made for the nearby shore. Here they later surrendered to a naval landing party.

The aftermath was the award of a DFC to Flt Lt Mitchell and a DFM to Sgt Stevenson; while the U-boat commander and two of his senior officers were eventually sentenced to death by a military court in Hamburg after the war for the murder of British and Allied seamen from the steamer *Peleus*, which U-852 had encountered only weeks before its ultimate action.

'Percolating' with 612 Squadron

Peter Brewster was a wireless operator (W/Op/AG) with 612 (County of Aberdeenshire) Squadron, Auxiliary Air Force (AAF), from March 1944 to February 1945:

'My crew was John Saul (skipper), Jack Church (second pilot), Jack Royans (Navigator), Bill Bates, Fred Floyer and myself, all W/Op/AGs, and we crewed up at 6 (C) OTU, Silloth, in November 1943, where we flew many of the earlier marks of Wimpy. On posting to 612 Squadron we began flying Leigh Light Wimpys fitted with Mk 3a radar, initially operating from Chivenor over the English Channel

Designed without any official support and under great secrecy by Wg Cdr Humphrey de Verd Leigh, the Leigh Light first entered service in 1942. (Crown Copyright via Martyn Chorlton)

and the Bay of Biscay, covering the D-Day operations. The radar was quite unique in those days, being a radial time-base with aerial situated in the nose of the aircraft; the front turret having been removed and replaced with a single 0.50 Browning machine gun on a free mounting.

'The Leigh Light was hydraulically operated and lowered from the dorsal turret position about halfway along the fuselage, usually by the wireless operator. The operator, being the second pilot, when operating the Light, lay in the bomb-aimer's position, on top of the Light's batteries. The Wimpy was also fitted with a radio altimeter in order that an attack on any U-boat could be carried out accurately from a mere 50ft altitude.

'After D-Day, because of our sensitive radar, we were posted in September 1944 to Limavady, to combat the Schnorchel being used by U-boats in the Northwest Approaches. Our radar was capable of picking up an echo from what amounted to a drainpipe sticking out of the sea. Soon after, however, we moved again, this time on 18 December 1944 to Langham, where we adopted an anti-shipping role, operating from the Hook of Holland to the German coast, and attacking convoys, which were apparently supplying German forces in their attempt to break through the Allied lines in the 'Battle of the Bulge'. Again, the radar played an important role because not only was it accurate, but also released the bombs on to target automatically. The only problem was that the aircraft had to be flown at a maximum height of 1,250ft for the accuracy to be maintained. In this job we were supported by Beaufighters and Mosquitos with rockets and cannons of New Zealand squadrons when we carried out attacks known as 'Percolating'. In short, after bombing a convoy we called up the New Zealanders and, after laying an artificial moonpath, they would attack with their RP and cannons.'

E-Boat Ops

Also based at Langham, from November 1944 to May 1945, was Andrew Hendrie, a W/Op/AG with 524 Squadron:

'I flew Wellington XIVs with 524 Squadron as a W/AG, with Fg Off Lister as captain for most trips. Operations were against E-boats, which would attempt, at night, and at an estimated 50 knots, to come over from the Dutch coast to the Humber estuary or off Harwich to attack our shipping. Our patrols were off Dan Helder, Ijmuiden, Rotterdam and Frisians. At briefings, therefore, areas of flak concentrations were usually stressed. We lost a lot of crews through aircraft going in too close to the coast. The first comment made to me by the squadron adjutant on joining 524 was, "Have you a car? There are so many here, and the former owners are now unknown." We had a Wellington detachment at Dallachy, home of a Beaufighter strike wing, whose role was to act as pathfinders by circling an enemy convoy, dropping a series of flares, to light the way for the Beau boys. At least, this was the proposal towards a three-squadron Beaufighter strike, escorted by Mustangs, which went to Norway. The Mustang 'escort' circled the wrong enemy fighter aerodrome; thankfully, the Wimpy's part was called off!

'I recorded only one successful attack against E-boats. This was on 6 April 1945 in Wimpy NB772, skipper Flt Lt Meggison, with take off from Langham at 00:45hrs. The wake of E-boats could be seen easily in bright moonlight, giving an indication of their speed. We found three of them. We gained height to about 6,000ft, the minimum specified altitude, otherwise we'd blow ourselves up too. If memory serves me, we dropped a stick of six 250lb bombs, intended to explode in mid-air and provided a wide 'shrapnel' effect. The E-boats would almost certainly have seen us, despite our black camouflage, in the bright moonlight, and they opened up with their single cannons fitted in the stern of each craft. We were hit only once when there was a brilliant flash near the rear turret. The gunner hadn't fired, he wanted to keep our position secret, and we thought we'd lost him. On return to base, we found quite a neat hole in the tail plane, which had missed the elevator mechanism by merely an inch or so.

Vickers Wellington GR Mk XIV, MP818 during trials at the A&AEE, Boscombe Down. The aircraft later served with 36 Squadron in the Mediterranean before joining Coastal Command at Chivenor and finally Benbecula, off the west coast of Scotland, until the unit was disbanded on 4 June 1945. The aircraft was then placed in temporary storage before being sold to the French Armée de l'Air in September 1946.

The purposeful Wellington GR Mk XIV, MP714 during performance and weapons trials in the hands of A&AEE test pilots out of Boscombe Down in Wiltshire. The aircraft was equipped with a Leigh Light in the ventral position within an extendible radome. (Via Martyn Chorlton)

Chapter 6

'Ake Ake Kia Kaha'

Born on 14 June 1919, in Wanganui, James Allen 'Jimmy' Ward was the son of English parents, devout Baptists who had moved to New Zealand from Coventry a few years earlier. 'Jimmy' was passionate about his new homeland, immersing himself in its diverse landscape and culture, which included learning Maori. Never more happy than when he was outdoors, Jimmy was a natural at sports, particularly rugby, tennis and swimming. As a young lad, Jimmy was an enthusiastic aero-modeller, a hobby that he continued until the end of his education.

The latter began at the Wanganui Technical College where Jimmy opted for an academic career, being accepted into the Teacher Training College in Wellington. Another future pilot, by the name of Edgar Kain (more familiarly known as 'Cobber' Kain) also briefly passed through the same training college, later going on to achieve great success during the Battle of France, only to die in a needless display of aerobatics over his airfield. Jimmy completed his education at Victoria University College, beginning his teaching career at Castle Cliff School in Wanganui in 1939. However, the war in Europe was brewing and Jimmy, like so many other young men from New Zealand, volunteered for the Royal New Zealand Air Force (RNZAF).

Left: **Sgt James Allen Ward VC, Royal New Zealand Air Force (RNZAF), standing on the pilot's seat of his 75 (NZ) Squadron at RAF Feltwell, in the summer of 1941.**

Below: **An enthusiastic aero-modeller during his youth, a trim 18-year old 'Jimmy' Ward poses with one of his flying models.**

Ward flew several operations as second pilot to Sqn Ldr R P Widdowson, RCAF, including the raid displayed on this operations board when 57 and 75 New Zealand (NZ) Squadrons attacked Düsseldorf, Germany. Flying Wellington Mk IC, R1457 'P', Widdowson's name can be seen eleventh from the top.

A publicity photograph of 'Jimmy' Ward and five of his crew at RAF Feltwell in late July 1941.

Photographs of L7818 appeared in the squadron's operations record book (ORB) clearly show the holes made in the Wellington's fabric by Ward as he inched towards the fire, which concentrated to the left of the starboard engine nacelle. Air 27/645 (National Archives)

Shy and unassuming, 'Jimmy' Ward wears his single VC ribbon on his tunic in August 1941. Sadly, he was lost over Hamburg on 15–16 September 1941 when the Wellington he was captain of was hit by flak.

75 (New Zealand) Squadron

Jimmy Ward was selected as a pilot and enlisted on 1 July 1940, beginning his basic training the same day at Levin Initial Training Wing. Flying training began on 29 July at No.1 EFTS at Taieri, with more advanced training following at Wigram. Jimmy earned his wings on 18 January 1941, and after being promoted to sergeant, enjoyed a few days leave before embarking aboard the *Aorangi* bound for Canada.

After arriving in Britain in March 1941, Ward was posted to 20 OTU at Lossiemouth before being posted to his first operational unit, 75 (New Zealand) Squadron, stationed at RAF Feltwell. His knowledge of Maori would mean that he would have recognised the squadron motto, 'Ake Ake Kia Kaha' as meaning 'For ever and ever be strong', which would have struck a chord with the young kiwi, whose parents' strong faith instilled in him the need to carry out his duty and look after those around him; both of which would have been good traits for a future Vickers Wellington captain. 75 (NZ) Squadron had only been reformed at Feltwell on 8 April 1940 with the Wellington Mk I, the geodetic creation of Barnes Wallis and one of the early pillars of Bomber Command.

Ward arrived at Feltwell on 13 June 1941, the day before his 22nd birthday, and it was not long before he was detailed as a second pilot to gain experience before he had a crew of his own. Over the coming weeks, Ward flew five operations with experienced Canadian, Sqn Ldr R. P. Widdowson in Wellington Mk IC, R1457 'P'. However, Widdowson was issued with a new aircraft, L7818, coded 'AA-R' on 7 July, and he and his crew only had time to carry out a 15-minute test flight before the bomber was being prepared for that nights' raid.

'Routine' trip to Münster

The night of 7–8 July 1941 was a reasonably busy one for Bomber Command with 114 Wellingtons detailed to attack Cologne, 54 Whitleys and 18 Hampdens allocated to Osnabrück, 40 Hampdens heading for Mönchengladbach and 49 Wellingtons ordered to bomb Münster. Sqn Ldr Widdowson, with Jimmy Ward as second pilot would be flying one of ten Wellingtons contributed by 75 (NZ) Squadron that night for the trip to Münster. Their crew for the operation were New Zealanders, Sgt L A Lawton, the navigator and Sgt A J R Box the rear gunner. Sgt W Mason, a Lincolnshire man, was the Wireless Operator and operating the front turret was Welshman, Sgt T Evans.

Laden with a 4,500lb bomb load, Widdowson lifted L7818 from Feltwell's grass runway at 23:10hrs, settling the bomber into a steady climb out over East Anglia and the North Sea beyond. The flight to the target was one of the quietest Ward had experienced so far and, apart from a few searchlights and some light flak, the bombing of Münster could only be described as 'routine'. After a successful bomb run, Widdowson made one circuit of the target before setting course for home.

Ward was standing peering out of the Wellington's astrodrome, keeping a good look out all around during the run over the Zuider Zee at 13,000ft. It was a crisp clear night with the moon shining bright and the comforting vision of the Dutch coast approaching ahead. However, Ward suddenly spotted the tell-tale shape of a Messerschmitt Bf110 night fighter approaching from the port, which had been stalking the Wellington for several minutes. Ward immediately called on the intercom to warn Widdowson but the device had gone U/S and the first sign that the Canadian pilot had of the enemy machine was when its cannon shells began slamming into the bomber. Shells ripped open hydraulic lines causing the bomb bay doors to drop open, the undercarriage to half-extend, Sgt Mason's wireless set was reduced to a twisted, smouldering wreck and all of the crew's communications lines had been cut. Most alarming was the fire in the starboard wing, which had taken hold after a fuel line had been ruptured, the escaping fuel feeding the flames, five-feet long, which ran over the top of the fabric-covered wing. Red-hot shrapnel rattled around the fuselage thankfully missing all six aircrew with the exception of the rear gunner, Sgt A Box who was wounded in the foot by a small piece.

Widdowson instinctively pushed the nose of the bomber down as the attack began, to dive clear of the enemy predator. Because of the damaged communication lines, the crew were unaware that the 19-year old rear gunner, Sgt Box, had engaged the Bf110 from almost point-blank range with his four .303in machine guns. As the Bf110 banked away from its initial attack, Box opened fire; the twin-engined fighter rolled on to its back and dived away, trailing smoke and never to be seen again.

Don parachutes

All on board the Wellington were convinced that they would have to bail out, so parachutes were donned as Widdowson adjusted his course to run parallel with the Dutch coast. In response to Widdowson's cry of '…see if you can put out that bloody fire', the crew punched a hole in the side of the fabric-covered fuselage to get better access to the burning wing. Fire extinguishers were tried but the slipstream and the distance of the fire out on the wing made these ineffective. The crew even tried throwing coffee at the fire which missed but may have at least dampened the surrounding fabric. It was at this point that Widdowson had to make a decision, he shouted, 'What does it look like to you?' Ward calmly replied, '…the fire doesn't seem to be gaining at all and it seems to be quite steady'. This reply made Widdowson's mind up, 'I think we'd prefer a night in the dinghy in the North Sea to ending up in a German prison camp', and with that the Canadian pilot turned the burning bomber north-east towards the English coast.

Pondering the situation, Ward decided to try and improve the odds of the Wellington getting back to Feltwell. To the astonishment of Sgt Lawton, Ward picked up the cockpit cover canvas and said, 'Think I'll hop out with this'. Ward takes up what happened next in his own words: 'I had a good look at the fire and I thought there was a sporting chance of reaching it by getting out through the astrodome, then down the side of the fuselage and out on to the wing. Joe, the navigator, said he thought it was crazy. There was a rope there; just the normal length of rope attached to the rubber dinghy to stop it drifting away from the aircraft when it's released on the water. We tied that round my chest, and I climbed up through the astrodome. I still had my parachute on. I wanted to take it off because I thought it would get in the way, but they wouldn't let me. I sat on the edge of the astrodome for a bit with my legs still inside, working out how I was going to do it. Then I reached out with one foot and kicked a hole in the fabric so that I could get my foot into the framework of the plane, and then I punched another hole through the fabric in front of me to get a hand-hold, after which I made further holes and went down the side of the fuselage on to the wing. Joe was holding on to the rope so that I wouldn't sort of drop straight off.

I went out three or four feet along the wing. The fire was burning up through the wing rather like a big gas jet, and it was blowing back just past my shoulder. I had only one hand to work with getting out, because I was holding on with the other to the cockpit cover. I never realised before how bulky a cockpit cover was. The wind kept catching it and several times nearly blew it away and me with it. I kept bunching it under my arm. Then out it would blow again. All the time, of course, I was lying as flat as I could on the wing, but I couldn't get right down close because of the parachute in front of me on my chest. The wind kept lifting me off the wing. Once it slapped me back on to the fuselage again, but I managed to hang on. The slipstream from the engine made things worse. It was like being in a terrific gale, only much worse than any gale I've ever known in my life.

I can't explain it, but there was no sort of real sensation of danger out there at all. It was just a matter of doing one thing after another and that's about all there was to it.

I tried stuffing the cockpit cover down through the hole in the wing on to the pipe where the fire was starting from, but as soon as I took my hand away the terrific draught blew it out again and finally it blew away altogether. The rear gunner told me afterwards that he saw it go sailing past his turret. I just couldn't hold on to it any longer.

After that there was nothing to do but to get back again. I worked my way back along the wing, and managed to haul myself up on to the top of the fuselage and got to sitting on the edge of the astrodome again. Joe kept the dinghy rope taut all the time, and that helped. By the time I got back I was absolutely done in. I got partly back into the astro-hatch, but I just couldn't get my right foot inside. I just sort of sat there looking at it until Joe reached out and pulled it in for me. After that, when I got inside, I just fell straight on to the bunk and stayed there for a time.'

With the main blaze now out, just as the bomber approached the Suffolk coast, the fire suddenly blazed up again as the final remnants of fuel that had pooled on the lower surface of the wing ignited. Luckily, the fire quickly burnt itself out and all thoughts now turned to getting the bomber down safely. Widdowson chose to land at the larger airfield at Newmarket, destined to be 75 (NZ) Squadron's station from November 1942 to June 1943. The crew hand pumped the undercarriage down and after Widdowson called Newmarket up saying 'We've been badly shot up. I hope we shan't mess up your flare-path too badly when we land,' the bomber touched down at 04:30hrs. Without flaps or brakes the bomber covered the large grass airfield quickly before coming to halt, aided by a barbed-wire fence and hedge beyond the end of the runway. L7818 was in such a state that the Wellington was declared a write-off, having flown one operational sortie.

Whisked off the short distance by road back to Feltwell, the crew was debriefed by the Intelligence Officer (IO) before heading for their billets.

'Awards Recommended'

After receiving a copy of the IOs report, the officer commanding 75 (NZ) Squadron, Wg Cdr C E Kay DFC began his regular ritual of relating a summary of the night's operations for official records. After reading the incredible story of what took place only a few hours earlier over the Dutch coast, Kay wrote in the 'Awards Recommended' column of his document, 'Widdowson – DFC, Box – DFM' and without hesitation, 'Ward – VC'. All of Kay's award recommendations were fully approved, Ward's VC being publicly announced in the *London Gazette* on 5 August 1941.

A very shy man, Ward found the adulation he received, especially by all who served on the squadron and station, hard to take. Whenever he was pressured into making a speech, Jimmy would always pay tribute to the ground crew or try and deflect attention away from himself.

Now first pilot of his own Wellington, it was particularly tragic that this brave young kiwi was destined to die on the night of 15–16 September 1941 when his aircraft, Wellington Mk IC, X3205 was hit repeatedly by flak over Hamburg. Sgt James Allen Ward, VC (401793) lies alongside three of his crew in Hamburg Cemetery (5A.A1.9).

Wellington Mk IA, N3006, nearing completion at Weybridge in the autumn of 1939 prior to delivery to 99 Squadron based at Newmarket. The bomber's service career was destined to be short because after being recalled because of poor weather conditions the bomber crashed on return to Newmarket at 22.25hrs at Chalk Hill, Barton Mills, Suffolk on 3 March 1940. All six crew were killed. (*Aeroplane*)

BACK FROM X COUNTRY....

Remember that accidents occur more frequently to tired men.
And that a turning prop is just as effective as Jerry Flak.
Don't let your crew get out until the props have stopped !

AIR
DIAGRAM
2810

AUG 1943

PREPARED BY
MINISTRY OF
AIRCRAFT PRODUCTION
FROM INFORMATION
AIR
MINISTRY

The interior of one of RAF Bramcote's three Type C Hangars during 105 (Transport) Operational Training Unit's (OTU) tenure on 7 March 1945. The unit was formed on 5 April 1943 and tasked with training crews for airline transport squadrons with an initial establishment of 40 Wellingtons when flying training began in July 1943. By early 1945, the Mk Is were replaced by the Mk X, the majority of which are on display here as a variety of instructional airframes. (*Aeroplane*)

Chapter 7

The Archetypal Bomber OTU Airfield

I n 1941, the demand for fully trained night bomber crews was high, with Bomber Command desperately trying to make an impact on the outcome of World War Two. This demand required airfields, which would be dedicated to such a task and Hixon was one of many that were specifically built for this purpose. For many, Hixon is the perfect example of a bomber OTU (Operational Training Unit), a role that it performed for virtually all of its wartime existence.

Construction of the new airfield began in mid-1941 by Trollope and Cole. It was located between the villages of Stowe-by-Chartley and Hixon, hemmed in by the North Staffordshire (Euston and Manchester) and LNER Stafford and Uttoxeter railway lines. The land belonged to two farmers by the names of Marston and Jackson. Both were relocated but the Marston family was unfortunate because they were moved to a house in Blithfield, which was destined to become the site of a reservoir only ten years later. The railway severely restricted any expansion plans for the airfield, which was built with three runways at 1650, 1400, and 1200yds respectively. Only the latter runway, which ran in a

'Unlucky for some?' Possibly one of the most famous official photographs of a Bomber Command OTU taken during World War Two and, luckily for us, from the top of Hixon's control tower. Only three serials are visible out of the 13 aircraft that are parked in front of the hangars in early 1944. All were lost before the war's end; Wellington Mk III BK347 (nearest the camera) was lost on 21 April 1944, followed by DF640 (second from the camera), only six days later. Wellington Mk III BJ597 (fourth from the camera) was lost on 1 June 1944. How many more out of this line-up did not make it? (IWM via Hixon Local Historical Society)

north-north-west/south-south-east direction, had the scope to be made longer and this only equated to approximately 200yds. The main technical area was located on the south-eastern side of the airfield, literally on the edge of Hixon village. Four Type T2 hangars were built on the edge of the technical site and later a Type B1 was also constructed across New Road along with a clutch of 'pan-handle' dispersals. The latter, which totalled 30, were liberally spread around the perimeter of the airfield. Two incendiary bomb stores were constructed on the western edge of the airfield; one of them was located across the North Staffordshire railway line and the other near the airfield perimeter track. Additional bomb stores, including fuses, were stored on the northern side, while the main fusing point was built less than 500ft from Stowe-by-Chartley village. This meant there was not much margin for error if anything went wrong. Accommodation, while classed as temporary, catered for nearly 2,400 officers and airmen and 445 Women's Auxiliary Air Force (WAAF).

The scene was now set for occupation of Hixon and, on 10 May 1942, a Bomber Command circular announced that Hixon would be placed within 7 Group. This was changed the following day to 92 Group and Lichfield was appointed as the parent station. The first RAF personnel to arrive on 13 May 1942 were the opening-up party. They were followed by Flt Lt J L Girling who assumed command of the station. Wg Cdr H McC White replaced Girling a few days later. Wg Cdr White took over on 8 June and not long after was promoted to Group Captain to become the first official station commander of Hixon.

30 OTU

It was now time for Hixon's first flying unit to be formed and this began on 28 June 1942 with 30 OTU. The unit's main equipment was to be at least 30 Wellingtons and its role was to train night-bomber crews. Before the new unit had even received any aircraft, Hixon was temporarily elevated to parent station status on 6 July. A signal from HQ, Bomber Command, stated that Hixon would be in charge of a new airfield at Whitchurch Heath (later named Tilstock), where 81 OTU was being formed.

Many, if not all, of the Wellingtons received by 30 OTU, had already seen operational service with a Bomber Command squadron. The Wellington Ic was the first of its mark to serve at Hixon.

The newly posted ground personnel were prematurely excited when the first aircraft descended upon Hixon on 15 July 1942. The first, a Wellington Mk Ic, touched down on a partly finished runway, followed shortly afterwards by a second. The two weary bombers belonged to 12 OTU at Chipping Warden and were destined to become ground instructional trainers rather than being the first for 30 OTU. The local contractors had not yet erected any windsocks and the Wellingtons were guided in using an improvised smoke indicator and green Very lights. The same day, Hixon's controlling group changed to 93 Group, forming at Lichfield and remaining there until close to the war's end.

The Air Officer Commanding (AOC) training for Bomber Command and AOC of 93 Group, Air Vice Marshal (AVM) Capel, visited Hixon on 17 July. Despite not a single airworthy aircraft being available, he set a target date of 4 August for flying training to begin at the airfield.

The first of three Wellingtons, which were part of the planned establishment of 30 aircraft, arrived, once again from 12 OTU, on 23 July. More aircraft continued to arrive and the first batch of flying instructors followed on 28 and 29 July. With only seven airworthy Wellingtons now on strength, the first course of 29 aircrew pupils arrived on 8 August 1942. The start date set by AVM Capel was, perhaps, rather ambitious, and flying training did not begin until August 23. The same day, a second course arrived, consisting of 30 more aircrew pupils. 30 OTU was now up and running with plans to receive a new course every fortnight.

The first of many inevitable accidents to occur at Hixon took place on 11 September. Sgt Stitt in Wellington Mk Ic N2779 was carrying out circuits and landings and, on one particular approach, he came in too fast, overshot the runway, crossed the Euston to Manchester railway line and came to a rest in an adjacent field.

Into action

After Air Chief Marshal Arthur Harris took over as Commander-in-Chief of Bomber Command in February 1942, aircraft from OTUs were regularly called upon to participate in large raids over Germany. While many other crews cut their teeth flying 'Nickel' (leaflet dropping) raids over France, the first taste of frontline operations for 30 OTU occurred over Bremen on 13–14 September 1942. Hixon dispatched four Wellingtons on the raid, which involved 446 aircraft, many from other OTUs. While the raid was deemed a success from a collateral damage point of view, 21 aircraft were lost, 13 of them from OTUs. Hixon's small contribution were lucky, three aircraft attacked the target although a fourth failed to find it. Included in the raid was Plt Of B J Staniland in Wellington Mk Ic DV771 who bombed the target and landed at Swanton Morley. Plt Of R Edwards returned early with a faulty compass and landed at Tatenhill and Flt Sgt Coles bombed the primary target from 14,000ft and also landed at Tatenhill.

The Wellington Mk III began to supersede the tired Mk Ics from early 1943 at Hixon. This example is the prototype at the A&AEE, Boscombe Down, Wiltshire.

30 OTU were joined by 1686 Bomber Defence Flight Training (BDTF) in July 1943, operating the Curtiss Tomahawk. All six pilots belonging to the unit pose in front of the American-built fighters. (Hixon Local Historical Society)

Two nights later, four more aircraft were detailed to take part in a frontline Bomber Command operation. This time, the target was Essen, with 369 aircraft taking part on a target, which had proved costly and difficult to attack. 39 aircraft, equating to more than ten per cent of the force were lost, of which, once again, OTU aircraft took the brunt with 18 aircraft missing in action. The 30 OTU contingent all survived with one Wellington returning early with intercom trouble and difficulty in climbing.

While Hixon was not particularly overcrowded, a satellite airfield became available at Seighford. Originally, Wheaton Aston was proposed but this failed to materialise and Seighford was officially taken over by 30 OTU on 16 September 1942. The use of this additional airfield would pay dividends in the near future as the unit began to increase in size. For air-to-air firing training, 30 OTU had a pair of target tugs on strength. These were a Lysander and a Defiant TT Mk I, one of many which were converted at Pendeford.

'Nickels'

The first 'Nickel' raid took place from the airfield during the night of 24 October 1942. Sgt N E Burton flew the operation over north-western France, successfully dropping 700lb of leaflets. Burton and crew returned to Hixon safely, despite receiving the attention of local flak defences and searchlights.

30 OTU's first fatal accident took place within sight of the airfield at 20:50hrs on 31 October 1942. W/O W L Primrose, a unit flying instructor, with crew, took off in Wellington Ic Z1083 for a practice bombing exercise at night. On return to Hixon, Primrose overshot his first approach to land and, during

the climb to go round again, the bomber stalled at only 500ft. With no chance of recovery, the Wellington crashed at Grange Farm, Amerton, killing all on board.

The first of many Bullseye exercises began at Hixon on the night of 7–8 November with three aircraft taking part. Within a few weeks though, 30 OTU would send out an average of 12 aircraft at a time. Bullseyes were a good way of teaching aircrews to fly over long distances within a formation and over relatively safe territory. Nickels continued over France for the remainder of the year and long-distance navigation exercises, usually flown across the Irish Sea, became routine for the unit.

New Year 1943 began with an influx of aircraft and personnel from 25 OTU at Finningley, which was being disbanded. Between 1 and 19 January, large parties of technical personnel and 26 Wellington Mk IIIs with their crews were added to 30 OTU's strength. The majority of the personnel and several aircraft were immediately transferred to Seighford. By the end of the month, 30 OTU had swelled to more than 2,800 personnel and 57 aircraft.

One airman was very lucky to survive when he accidentally walked into the revolving propeller of Wellington Mk X HE428 on 2 February 1943. These accidents were considered inevitably fatal but the accident report simply states that 'the propeller was badly damaged'!

Up until December 1942, the unit had been solely equipped with the Wellington Ic, the majority of which were becoming very tired. HQ Bomber Command made the decision that 30 OTU should be totally re-equipped with the Wellington Mk III and X, of which several had already arrived on the unit. In February 1943, the unit held 35 Wellington Mk IIIs, 15 Wellington Xs and only six Wellington Ics; the latter had already been allotted to other units.

10 April 1943 was a day to forget for 30 OTU when two aircraft were lost at dawn within 15 minutes of each other. The first accident involved Wellington Mk III BK179, which crashed, five minutes after take-off, into Ranton Woods, close to the airfield. The pilot, Flg Off R Haynes and four crewmembers were killed instantly. The second, Wellington Mk III DP611, lost power 40 minutes after take-off and the pilot, Flt Sgt R A Jones, decided to force land on a straight piece of road near Hartington. All went well, until moments before the bomber slid to a halt. The Wellington struck a solid wall, splitting open one of the bomber's fuel tanks and then quickly burst into flames. Only two of the five crew escaped.

With more aircraft available and an increase in aircrew courses passing through Hixon, the unit was able to increase the amount of Wellingtons sent on Nickel operations. On average, three Nickels were being flown every month, with at least eight aircraft on each. The crews that were sent on these raids were generally near the end of their OTU training and recorded statistics for the unit show that very few were lost during these forays over enemy territory.

Planning the training curriculum at Hixon was becoming increasingly difficult as the unit grew in size. Divided into four flights, trainee aircrew within a flight could be at one of four stages of their training and it was obvious that the schedule needed simplifying. The solution was straightforward, on arrival at Hixon, each crew would be allocated a flight and would stay with it until the end of their training. Known as a 'straight-through' training system, the flight simply changed its function as each new stage of training was reached. With the AOCs for the group's authority, the new system began in April 1943 and remained in place until 30 OTU disbanded.

May 1943 was one of the busiest for Nickel operations over France. Five Nickels were flown and all but one managed to drop their cargo into the correct target area. Despite the unit being equipped with slightly newer aircraft, they were no less susceptible to technical malfunctions. On 24–25 May, outbound to France, Sgt P A J Shoreland had to turn back when he was 35 miles south of Leicester because the bomb doors would not open and failed oxygen equipment.

More Nickels were carried out in June, with the main targets now being Paris, Lorient, Brest and Nantes. It was during a raid on the latter that 30 OTU lost its first aircrew on a Nickel operation.

A Tomahawk takes off from a snowy Hixon during the winter of 1943/44. If the runway could be cleared then the aircraft would fly. (Hixon Local Historical Society)

Three aircraft, including Wellington Mk III BK559, piloted by Flt Sgt T G Dellar RAAF, were tasked with a Nickel raid on Nantes. Dellar and his crew became lost and, at 03:30hrs, after dropping their bundles of leaflets, set course for home while very low on fuel. Still uncertain of their position and with fuel at a critical level, Dellar gave the order for his crew to bale out. Three complied, but Flt Sgt D M Davis RCAF stayed with Dellar who did not have a parachute. It is believed that the Wellington came down near Versailles. Flt Sgt Dellar is alleged to have died in the crash and Davies is thought to have been killed while evading capture, as his grave is several hundred miles away, near Marseilles. Of the three who bailed out, two became POWs and a third, Sgt B C Reeves, managed to evade capture.

The biggest single Nickel operation from Hixon took place on 22–23 June 1943. Sixteen aircraft took part: ten Wellingtons targeted Paris, two Orleans, two Le Mans and two were given Reims. One aircraft returned early with technical problems and another landed at West Malling after the starboard engine caught fire off Beachy Head. One aircraft, Wellington Mk X HE527, piloted by Flg Sgt J Hennessy RAAF, was reported missing and it was later discovered that the bomber had been hit by flak over Cherbourg.

The Wellington X was the most prolific mark of this famous bomber ever produced. 30 OTU received its first example in early 1943.

The main equipment of 12 Pilots Advanced Flying Unit (PAFU) was three different marks of the Bristol Blenheim, including the Blenheim IV depicted here.

Fighter affiliation

30 OTU received its own fighter affiliation unit when 1686 Bomber (Defence) Training Flight (BDTF) was formed at Hixon on 1 July 1943. 1686 BDTF was the sixth unit to be formed and the second within 93 Group. All were equipped with the American-built Tomahawk single-seat fighter, known in the US as the P-40. Virtually all of the Tomahawks on the BDTFs had served and seen action in North Africa with several hours on the clock. They were ideal for fighter affiliation and proved a useful asset to the unit. 1686 BDTF had six aircraft on strength, made up of four Tomahawk Is (AH783, 832, 850 and 852), a single IIA (AH926) and IIB (AK128).

The loss and accident rate on Bullseye exercises were beginning to exceed all of the other operations combined from the airfield. A typical example occurred on the night of 6–7 July when six aircraft took off from Hixon for a Bullseye. On their return to the airfield at 03:44hrs, Wellington Mk X HE328 crashed near Hanging Wicket, approximately two miles east of the airfield after losing control in cloud. The pilot, Flg Off A Beare, and his crew of five were killed. One of those killed was Second Lt T E Fenwick who was attached from 154 Heavy Anti-Aircraft Regiment, Royal Artillery.

Northern France

On 30–31 August 1943, for the first time in Hixon's short history, aircraft from the unit would take part in a major bombing raid against the enemy. 33 OTU Wellingtons, four of them from Hixon, were tasked with attacking an ammunition dump at Forêt d'Eperlecques, north of St Omer, Northern France. This was the first of a series of small raids, specifically arranged for OTU crews, where Pathfinder Mosquitoes marked the target. The experience gained by bombing a marked target would be useful once they were posted on to a frontline squadron. The major distraction of a 660 aircraft raid on Mönchengladbach the same night helped keep the enemy away from the OTU raid. Three 30 OTU Wellingtons dropped a total of 16 500lb bombs while the fourth aircraft, failing to see the target markers, jettisoned its bomb load into the channel. The attack on the dump was successful with a large explosion being witnessed by many of the crews. Hixon's contingent returned home safely but two Wellingtons were lost from other OTUs.

Four more aircraft were detailed again from Hixon on 31 August–1 September to attack another ammunition dump in Northern France. The same night, Bomber Command launched another big raid against Germany with 622 aircraft attacking Berlin. The considerably smaller force, which consisted of 30 Wellingtons, six Pathfinder Mosquitoes and five Halifaxes, set out to bomb the dump at Forêt de Hesdin. Two Wellingtons from Hixon dropped a total of 16 500lb bombs on the target, but two others, failing to see the target, jettisoned their bombs into the sea. Once again, the raid was a success, without loss, in stark contrast to the Berlin raid, which was deemed a failure with 47 aircraft failing to return.

A third and final trip to bomb targets in Northern France took place on 2–3 September with two Wellingtons from Hixon taking part. Thirty Wellingtons with six Pathfinder Mosquitoes and five Lancasters marking, bombed the ammunition dump at Forêt de Mormal. Sgt K L Perry in Wellington Mk X HE413 dropped seven 500lbs bombs on to the target while Plt Off J Hart jettisoned the same size load into the channel. This was another successful trip for all concerned, without loss.

On the night of 8–9 September 1943, Bomber Command gathered a mixed force of 257 aircraft to attack a German long-range gun battery at Boulogne. Several Wellingtons from OTUs contributed aircraft: in Hixon's case, three bombers took part. This particular raid also had five USAAF B-17s taking part. This was the first time that American aircraft had flown alongside Bomber Command aircraft during a night-bombing sortie. Two out of three of the 30 OTU Wellingtons claimed to have bombed the target, while a third, BJ986, flown by Sgt A J Sandford, returned early and dropped its bomb over Cannock range. Post attack reconnaissance revealed that poor marking by the Pathfinder Mosquitoes resulted in the gun battery being undamaged.

One of the last military aircraft to operate en masse from Hixon was the Beaufort trainer of 12 PAFU. It was operated in the Coastal Command camouflage scheme as displayed on this example.

One of a series of aerial photographs taken of Hixon on 11 August 1945. By this time, the airfield is devoid of aircraft and 16 Maintenance Unit (MU) is in residence. The two subsidiary runways have received a white cross, indicating that they are closed while the main runway remains open. (Crown Copyright via Hixon Local Historical Society)

Personnel of 16 MU pose for the camera at Hixon in 1948. (Hixon Local Historical Society)

Hixon's Type 12779 control tower is preserved in excellent condition and serves the airfield as the site's main office.

Aerial view of the airfield taken in the early 1990s, showing the main runway and a second, shorter runway still intact. Many airfield buildings survive, the vast majority of them are still in daily use. Hixon village is at the bottom right, having almost quadrupled in size since World War Two.

30 OTU's role within Bomber Command was extended slightly from 13 January 1944. Despite being quite a few miles from the nearest coastline, Hixon's aircraft were now called upon to carry out Air Sea Rescue (ASR) operations, specifically over the North Sea, looking for ditched crews returning from raids on Germany. Six aircraft took part in the first ASR sortie to search for missing Lancaster Mk III ED826 of 15 Squadron at Mildenhall, which was later discovered to have crashed into the sea, 13 miles south of Skegness.

British Empire Medal

A routine practice circuit and bump exercise, in the afternoon, on 10 February, resulted in a local workman performing an unselfish act of bravery. Sgt W E Keeler in Wellington Mk X HF516 had his starboard engine cut while at only 1,000ft. Rapidly losing height, Wheeler attempted to land on one of the shorter subsidiary runways. The Wellington did not make the runway and came down, wheels up, in a field south of New Road. The bomber swung to starboard, crashing into a concrete mixer and a pile of gravel being used for the construction of the B1 hangar near the road. After a few tense moments, the crew began scrambling clear of the bomber, which began to catch fire. Sgt A J Welstead, the Wireless Operator, was making his escape but his parachute harness became hooked up. One of the contractors working on the hangar, Mr Cyril Fradley, ran to the burning bomber and dragged Welstead clear. Sadly, Sgt Welstead was badly burned and succumbed to his injuries in Stafford General Hospital the following day. Cyril Fradley, for his bravery, was awarded the British Empire Medal (BEM).

The Wellingtons of 30 OTU were becoming very tired by early 1944, and the unserviceability rate was increasing daily. On almost every 'Bullseye' exercise during the year at least one aircraft returned with a technical problem or was lost as a result of one. Of the eight aircraft that took part in a Special Command Bullseye from Hixon on 11 February, half of them had technical problems. These ranged from engine trouble, magneto drops and oil leaks to an unserviceable sextant. On 16 February, only four aircraft took part in a Bullseye and all struggled back to Hixon with major technical problems.

Six Wellingtons from 'D' Flight took part in a Nickel raid in the Orleans area of Northern France on 9–10 May. One aircraft, Wellington Mk III BJ618, flown by Flt Lt R C Thorn, failed to return and hopes were not high for the crew's survival. Whether the aircraft suffered from a mechanical failure or was hit by flak is unknown but all of the crew survived after the bomber crashed near Selles, 6km south of Pont-Audemer. In fact, four, including Thorn, managed to evade capture while two others became POWs. Another Wellington diverted to Tarrant Rushton after the navigator became ill. The others returned to Hixon but Sgt Bowater's arrival in Wellington Mk X LN533 was more spectacular than planned. The bomber was already having problems with its intercom but this problem became secondary after what seemed to be a standard landing. Immediately after touchdown, the Wellington burst into flames. Bowater steered the bomber off the main runway, the crew promptly vacated the burning aircraft and the emergency services were quickly on the scene extinguishing the fire. Despite the apparent ferocity of the fire, the aircraft was not seriously damaged and was quickly repaired, going on to serve with 11 AGS until March 1948.

Bullseyes

August 1944 was dominated by more Special Command Bullseyes. Since the allied invasion, Nickels over Northern France had come to an end simply because of the odds of being shot down, which had dramatically increased. While a group of aircraft were taking part in a Bullseye on 26 August, Plt Off Mettrick in Wellington Mk X LP570 overshot the runway. The bomber came to rest on the LNER railway line with its undercarriage damaged but the crew was uninjured. The five aircraft taking part in the

Bullseye were diverted to Seighford, which was not an unusual occurrence, but was an inconvenience for the crews. That same evening, the ground personnel were involved in moving another bomber away from the railway line. While, on night circuits and landings, Flt Sgt R E George in Wellington Mk X HE224 touched the runway too fast, ballooned back into the air, overshot the runway and crashed in virtually the same position as LP570 had done only hours before. The bomber was seriously damaged but the crew was unhurt. Because of the high probability of an aircraft crashing on the railway line, special phone lines were laid between signal boxes so that signalmen could be informed as soon as a crash took place.

Bullseye exercises continued to be the main activity with up to 14 Wellingtons taking part at a time. Accidents continued to occur throughout the summer of 1944, as the Wellington Mk III and X were becoming tired and prone to mechanical failures. As with the earlier Mk Is, hydraulic and electrical failures became the most common reasons why an aircraft had to divert and carry out an emergency landing during a training sortie.

During October, the unit was reduced to three-quarters status with a reduced establishment of 40 Wellingtons and five Hurricanes. This was seen as an early indication that the demand for night-bomber crews was dwindling despite Bomber Command still suffering alarming losses on raids over Germany. This reduction in status also meant that Seighford was no longer needed, and on October 28, the satellite airfield was relinquished to Flying Training Command.

The final Bullseye operation that 30 OTU participated in took place on 2 December. Five aircraft of 'A' Flight took part in the operation, and all returned safely to Hixon without any unserviceabilities reported. It is quite possible that this was one of the last Bullseye operations mounted by the OTU units during World War Two.

Twelve aircraft were detailed to take part in Operation *Sweepstake* on 14–15 January; the last significant operation that 30 OTU would take part in from Hixon. The operation involved 126 aircraft, all from bomber OTUs, as a flying diversion over the North Sea to distract the enemy from frontline Bomber Command operations. The operation for many of the bombers involved using up more fuel than anticipated and four of Hixon's Wellingtons were diverted to Topcliffe, another to Catfoss, both Yorkshire. Flg Off P N Hickman was ordered to divert but could not find a gap in cloud cover. At 00:20hrs the tanks ran dry and Hickman ordered his crew to bale out. Hickman followed soon after and the bomber crashed on to tennis courts at Wilford, south of the River Trent, on the southwest side of Nottingham. Ten minutes later, another Hixon machine was being abandoned near Nottingham. Flt Sgt D Hudson in Wellington Mk X LP830 had also run short of fuel and his crew successfully abandoned their aircraft. One member of this crew, complete with parachute under his arm, caught a bus from Arnold into Nottingham. A local farmer rescued another airman after he was caught up in the branches of a tree bordering the Henry Mellish Grammar School rugby football ground. These two aircraft losses were the last to be suffered by 30 OTU while at Hixon.

Plans were already in place for a large reshuffle of units throughout the country and this included Hixon. 30 OTU's move from Hixon was carried out with great efficiency; the advance party of 16 Officers, 28 NCOs and 145 other ranks began to leave on 25 January. The destination was Gamston, which had not long supported a bomber-training unit of its own until 86 OTU was disbanded in October 1944. The main move day occurred on 2 February 1945 when 41 Wellingtons, 167 Officers, four WAAF Officers, 774 Other Ranks, 198 RAF Sgt Aircrew and 314 WAAF other ranks departed Hixon for the final time. The 55th training course was continued at Gamston. The station commander Gp Cap F F Rainsford honoured 30 OTU with the following comment in the unit's Operational Record Book: *"Although this unit has closed for the best of reasons – the end of the European War – its dissolution will be felt by many. The cheerfulness, enthusiasm and sterling work of all ranks achieved a spirit which will be an inspiration for the tasks of peace."*

Closed but not forgotten

While Gp Capt Rainsford's words indicated a closure of 30 OTU, the unit was not disbanded until 12 June, but their most important work will always be seen as occurring at Hixon.

Only a few days later, Hixon gained a new unit with the arrival of 12 (Pilots) Advanced Flying Unit (PAFU) from Spittlegate. 12 PAFU's equipment was approximately 60 Blenheim Mk Is, IVs and Vs plus Oxfords, Ansons, a Whitney Straight, Moth and Proctors in support. The war's end at Hixon brought flying almost to a halt and, on 21 June 12 PAFU's short time at the airfield came to an end with disbandment. All of the unit's aircraft were flown out to various Maintenance Units (MU) throughout the country; the Beauforts were flown to 44 MU at Edzell in Scotland, for storage and eventual scrapping.

The vast Equipment Supply Depot at 16 MU Stafford was in desperate need of sub-sites to cope with the vast influx of surplus military items. Hixon was chosen as one of seven sub-sites for 16 MU; the unit taking up residence on 31 July. The MU remained until 5 November 1957, when Hixon was reduced to Care and Maintenance. The Air Ministry sold the airfield in August 1962, dividing the airfield up between farming and light industrial units on the old technical site.

Today, Hixon is without doubt Staffordshire's best-preserved wartime airfield with many buildings still in existence and in daily use. Three out of the original four Type T2 hangars are still in use and the Type B1 on the south side of New Road has had a face lift with a modern business façade. The entire main runway is still intact and large sections of one of the subsidiary runways are also in place. The entire perimeter is virtually complete and large sections are now a public footpath. Another object that remains is a windsock pole on the north side of the airfield and the Type 12779 control is also preserved.

Many of the dispersed site buildings also still remain around the village; once again many are used for private dwellings or light industrial purposes. Every building still standing on the original airfield technical site is occupied by a business, two of which are aviation-related and airframes including helicopters are parked within the site.

Chapter 8

Holding Their Arm

The *Top Gun* philosophy behind the Central Gunnery School (CGS) in World War Two can be summed up quite simply. To be successful at anything requires the process of learning to be continuous. If learning ceases, failure sets in. In 'safe' occupations failure may be a slow process but for the air-gunner, especially in war, failure can be sudden, irreversible and even fatal, not only for himself but possibly for his crew too. If this holds true for the air-gunner in the turret of a bomber, it is equally relevant for the pilot of a fighter aeroplane. All the pilot's skill is of little use if his shots go wide of the target. A gunner can only retain his expertise by constant practice; by continually getting to grips with new problems resulting from new air tactics, improved aircraft performance or increased armour protection on his opponents. Much of the knowledge necessary to keep standards high comes from the experiences of others who have already proved their ability in these fields. Furthermore, if the first-hand experience passed on is gleaned from a succession of such 'teachers', then that knowledge keeps pace with current developments in the field of combat and at both tactical and command levels. Recognising this need for continued and advanced instruction, the RAF, in addition to its ordinary air gunnery training schools, established a CGS after which those trained would return to their squadrons to impart new techniques and tactics to other aircrew colleagues. Formed on 6 November 1939 under the command of Gp Capt W H Poole AFC MM, Warmwell, Dorset, was the first home for CGS and although not the only bomber type used, the Vickers Wellington was soon to become the mainstay of its operations.

When CGS 'Gunnery Leader (Bomber) Wing' arrived at Sutton Bridge (Lincolnshire) from Chelveston (Northamptonshire) on 1 April 1942, it was equipped with the Vickers Wellington, the Handley Page Hampden and a few Lockheed Hudsons, although the latter pair was phased out by the end of 1942.

A well known and photographed Wellington was Mk IA N2887, pictured during service with the Central Gunnery School (CGS) at RAF Sutton Bridge in June 1943. The Weybridge-built bomber first joined 99 Squadron in 1940, followed by service with 11 and 15 OTU before joining the CGS. (*Aeroplane*)

In the meantime, fighter ace Wg Cdr A G 'Sailor' Malan received the go-ahead to create a separate Pilot Gunnery Instructor Wing at Wittering (Cambridgeshire) where, under the auspices of CGS, it was established but would shortly move its Spitfire, Mustang and Master aircraft to Sutton Bridge. It was a logical step for both elements of the CGS to be co-located to facilitate co-operation in their practical gunnery exercises and this is why the Gunnery Leader (Bomber) and the Pilot Gunnery Instructor Training courses both came to be at Sutton Bridge in April 1942. On 7 May, RAF Sutton Bridge saw the arrival of Gp Capt Claude Hilton Keith as station commander, bringing with him a fearsome reputation as an experienced bomber operations and gunnery training specialist. The AOC 25 (Armament) Group told him his new command was '...dirty, unhappy and inefficient' and Gp Capt Keith recalled: *"I flew to Sutton Bridge and confirmed the truth of this!"*

Training at the CGS was run on different lines to that encountered at the basic Air Gunnery schools. Gp Capt Keith clarified this difference by explaining that the CGS: *"...provided post-operational training for air gunners and fighter pilots. Its pupils were those who had already gained experience on active operations and shown themselves sufficiently successful to justify their being given an advanced course in air gunnery, lasting a period of one month."* Quite what were the criteria for being rated as 'sufficiently successful' is not explained. He continued: *"Each course catered for ten fighter pilots and 32 air gunners and with a 50 per cent overlap there were always twice those numbers of airmen on the station."*

Gunnery Leader Wing

CGS activity at Sutton Bridge began with Nos. 35 and 36 Gunnery Leaders (Bomber) courses and No. 5 Pilot Gunnery Instructors course – course Nos 1 to 4 having been held at Wittering.

Fighter boys went to the Fighter Wing under the command of the famous 'Sailor' Malan, ably assisted by his deputy and Chief Instructor, Sqn Ldr Allan Wright. According to Gp Capt Keith, Malan was a first-class exponent of air gunnery and lived up to it, but was not very interested in what the air gunners in the bombers did. These latter were trained by the Bomber Wing, commanded by Wg Cdr J M Warfield – ironically, an ex-Malta campaign fighter pilot – but he was succeeded on 25 June by an old hand on bombers, Wg Cdr J J Sutton. The purpose of the school was to turn out gunnery instructors to work in operational squadrons and training units – graduates of the Fighter Wing would be responsible for training pilots in all aspects of fixed gunnery training – and graduates of the Gunnery Leader Wing would be responsible for training air gunners and wireless operator/air gunners in all aspects of free gunnery training, with an emphasis on tactics. The duties and responsibilities of a newly qualified Gunnery Leader when he returned to his unit were:

1) To serve as an air gunner in the air and personally maintain a high standard of marksmanship.
2) To know and understand his air gunners, to stimulate their interest, improve their operational efficiency and maintain their morale; and to ensure their physical fitness.
3) To initiate and control training in gunnery and aircraft recognition.
4) To check, but not technically supervise, gun and turret maintenance and the harmonisation of sights.
5) To advise Air Gunners and other members of the Squadron on gunnery equipment and its uses.
6) To help Squadron and Flight Commanders in administration and disciplinary matters affecting Air Gunners.
7) To discuss, collate and explain all facts and principals relating to air-fighting tactics.

The Wellington bomber became the workhorse for these exercises and many of the 30 or so aircraft at the station were Mk IAs from early batches in the L and N series and had been in service since the war

began. Aerial combat sessions were carefully briefed and lasted about an hour. The bomber would have four pupils aboard whose initial exercises would be on range estimation followed by quarter attacks, then varied attacks. The latter included attacks from quarter, half-roll from above and from below, then all angles and head-on. Later stages of the course involved full evasive action by the bomber and all the variety of fighter attacks. Normally, these exercises took place at 3,000ft, but there would also be attacks on low-flying bombers. Of all these, the head-on exercises were the most dangerous because of the high closing speed. The initiative for these attacks lay with the fighter pilot who had to thoroughly work out his approach and, most importantly, his breakaway. At the end of the course the fighter pilots would have the chance to take a trip in a bomber and try out the turrets to give them an idea of the air gunner's point of view. Friendly rivalry abounded between the two Wings – the air gunners having the opportunity to test themselves against highly experienced staff fighter pilots (for example, the likes of George 'Screwball' Beurling!) and the most able pilots from operational fighter squadrons – leading to an exciting atmosphere for those involved. All of this was supported by the use of towed targets, courtesy of the Hawker Henley and Westland Lysander aircraft of the integral CGS Target Towing Flight.

Training was intensive and hard work for all concerned. Firstly, air practice for the gunners in the turrets and secondly, for the fire controller gunner who stood in the astrodome controlling and directing the aircraft's gunnery defences as well as giving orders to the pilot for evasive action. The instructor

The staff of the CGS Bomber Gunnery Leaders Wing at Sutton Bridge, Lincolnshire, in June 1943; from left to right, Flt Sgt V I Jones, W/O R C Hillebrandt, Fg Off W W Cumber, Flt Sgt H A Matthews, Sgt R F Crabb, Flt Sgt E Saunders, Gp Capt C E St J Beamish (Station Commander), Wg Cdr J C Claydon (OC CGS Bomber Wing), Sqn Ldr K M Bastin (Chief Instructor), Flt Lt W E Nicholas, Flt Lt M C Cleary, Flt Lt V W C Taylor, Flt Lt A J Savage, Plt Off R L A Woolgar, Flt Lt H S Griffiths, Plt Off E J Law and W/O E J Saunders. (*Aeroplane*)

taking the exercise would be in the second pilot's seat observing and listening on the intercom and the bomber pilots would not stint in throwing their aircraft around in response to evasion instructions. So violent were some manoeuvres – including the famous 'bomber corkscrew' – that often the Wellington was pulling two or three 'G' of gravity and, during one such energetic sortie, a pupil lost his footing while acting as fighting controller in a Wellington that corkscrewed away from a fighter attack and he finished up with a broken leg and minor facial injuries. Aerial combat exercises were carried out over the ranges in The Wash and above the surrounding Fenland and were briefed very carefully because of the dangers involved. The Chief Instructor or his deputy managed the exercise until the bomber took off, then the instructor in the bomber controlled it, but the risks of combat conditions could not be eliminated if the exercises were to be anything like realistic. Mistakes were almost inevitable and the threat of a mid-air collision was ever-present.

AC1 Douglas Broom, an engine fitter at CGS Sutton Bridge, recalled:

"All our 'kites' – bombers and fighters – were heavily used but with the relatively small size of the maintenance facilities available for such a large number of aeroplanes, serviceability was always a problem. On 9 December 1942, for example, even working flat out all day, we could still only get 20 aircraft serviceable out of 60 assorted aircraft on the 'drome. Our establishment of Wellingtons was around 30 aircraft but they were so old it was hard to get even a dozen of them ready for flying each day. My time at CGS drew to a sad close with a fatal crash between Wisbech and Huntingdon on 10 April 1943, when one of our Spitfires [P7677] was making a quarter-rear attack on a 'Wimpy' [N2865]. The pilot failed to pull out of his dive in time and ran into the rear turret of the Wellington, which crashed killing all six on board. The Spitfire pilot also crashed and was seriously injured. One of my last duties at CGS was to parade for the burial of one of the Wellington crew [pilot Flt Lt Terence Stanbury] in Sutton Bridge churchyard."

Above: Formed at Warmwell, Dorset, on 6 November 1939, the CGS moved to Castle Kennedy, southwest Scotland, and Chelveston, Northamptonshire before arriving at Sutton Bridge on 1 April 1942. This scene was taken at Chelveston between December 1941 and March 1942 showing a Wellington fuselage split down the middle, which would have proved useful as a teaching aid. (*Aeroplane*)

Left: CGS Bomber Wing staff W/O R C Hillebrandt (holding model Wellington) and Flt Lt M C Cleary (with model Spitfire) demonstrate a typical air-to-air firing exercise for the benefit of the press and a small, yet appreciative audience. (*Aeroplane*)

Miles of cine film were exposed by air gunners using camera guns fitted to their turrets and by fighter pilots alike, with exhaustive viewing and evaluation sessions after each sortie. Ground training also included the theory of ballistics, discussion of tactics, aircraft recognition and, later on, clay pigeon shooting – this latter was ideal for deflection training. Interestingly, instructors on the Bomber Wing found themselves constantly reminding their students that there was nothing wrong with the .303in machine gun as a defensive weapon – if used properly. Often they had to correct a common perception among the general ranks of air gunners that the maximum range of the .303in was 600yds; emphasising instead that '600yds' should be regarded as the opening range.

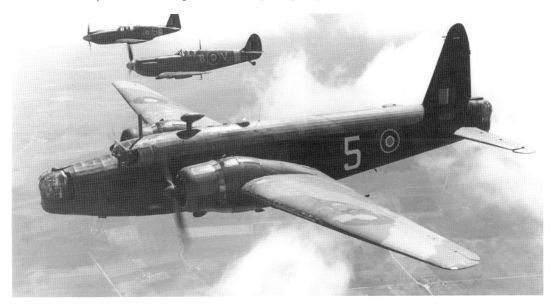

Above: Images of CGS aircraft are very rare, with the exceptions, of a series of air-to-airs taken by the celebrated photographer Charles E Brown in June 1943. The same Wellington Mk IA N2887, is now accompanied by a pair of nimble friends in the shape of a Spitfire Mk IIA and Mustang Mk I. (Via *Aeroplane*)

Right: Gp Capt Charles Beamish, flanked by the senior staff of the CGS Fighter Wing at Sutton Bridge, in June 1943. On his right is Sqn Ldr R C Dafforn, on his left is Wg Cdr P G R Walker, the CO of the Fighter Wing and on the right is Fg Off George 'Screwball' Beurling DSO, DFC, DFM. (*Aeroplane*)

Thousand-bomber raids

In May 1942, momentous events in the operational arena filtered down to training unit level when the Wellington bombers of CGS took a small slice of the action. Background to what became known as the 'Thousand bomber' raids is generally well known but how did the Wellington 'training hacks' of the CGS come to be involved in this attack?

In order to achieve his magic 1,000-aeroplane figure, 'Bomber' Harris had to pull in men and machines from every unit in Bomber Command, right down to the Command's own OTUs. When Coastal Command, which originally agreed to contribute 250 bombers, was ordered out of the raid by the Admiralty – the result of a long-running political argument between the two Services – Flying Training Command, of which CGS was a part, was also scoured for suitable aircraft. It is recorded that just four Wellingtons were contributed by Training Command, largely because most of that Command's bombers were either inadequately equipped for night-bombing operations or were so 'tired' that they were incapable of making a sustained journey. This is where CGS made its small contribution to the momentous Operation *Millennium*. The small quantity was indeed because by the time a Wellington reached CGS it was usually in a 'war weary' condition, having come off ops, and often lacked fully-functional instruments and equipment.

One such example was Wellington Mk IA, N2894. Delivered to the RAF in November 1939, this aircraft was one of 149 Squadron's contingent despatched on 18 December 1939 to attack Wilhelmshaven during what became known as the Battle of Heligoland Bight. It was one of two aircraft that turned back from that raid due to technical problems and was therefore fortunate to survive the subsequent loss of half of its comrades.

At CGS, these hand-me-down Wellingtons were serviced in a manner that just kept them airworthy for their diet of low-risk, short-duration, short-distance sorties trundling around relatively friendly airspace above The Wash and dealing with mock attacks by reasonably friendly Spitfires or firing at towed targets. When Harris's clarion call for aircraft came, only three CGS bombers could be repaired and serviced – with some cannibalised parts – in time to bring them up to a standard that would enable them to have a chance of staying in the air long enough to get to Cologne and back; to be able to communicate and also to defend themselves on the way – and N2894 was one of this little band.

On 26 May, three Wellingtons from CGS, including N2894, were detached to the nearby operational station RAF Feltwell '...for special operational co-operation with Bomber Command'. Staff pilots, wireless operators (from the WOp/AGs), air-gunners and complete ground crews were supplied by CGS on detachment for the few days around the raid date. When the attack began, these three CGS Wellingtons took off from Feltwell in company with 44 other Wellingtons; 20 from 57 Squadron, 23 from 75 Squadron and one aircraft from another unidentified Training Command unit. Forty one aircraft were lost that night from a total of 1,047 despatched and RAF Sutton Bridge took its share of those casualties too when Wellington Mk IA, N2894, of CGS was reported missing.

It was the last bomber to be despatched from Feltwell, at 23:47hrs on 30 May and was not heard from again. Four of the crew of six were members of CGS staff and there was a mood of sadness on the station for the loss of Plt Off David Johnson, the aircraft captain; Flt Sgt Josiah Connor, WOp/AG; Flt Sgt John McLean, air gunner; and Flt Sgt Gordon Waddington-Allwright, rear gunner. Acting as second pilot for the trip was WO Oldřich Jambor, a Czech pilot with 34 operations with 311 Squadron to his name – including 18 as aircraft captain. Having only recently finished a four-month spell of instructing, Jambor was posted back to ops with 75 Squadron at Feltwell, arriving just before the end of May. Not yet crewed-up, as a 'spare bod' he therefore found himself in this ropey old CGS Wellington for the 'big show', along with a spare navigator Flt Lt Hector Batten also from 75 Squadron. After the war it was discovered that, having successfully bombed Cologne, N2894 was shot down over Klaarenbeek, near Apeldoorn Holland, by a Messerschmitt Bf110 night fighter flown by the ace Oblt Helmut Woltersdorf of 7/NJG 1, one of his last 'kills' since he, too, died on 2 June as the result of crash-landing his battle-damaged Bf110.

With the exception of rear gunner Flt Sgt Waddington-Allwright, who bailed out and was made a POW, the remainder of the crew of N2894 died and are all buried in Ugchelan-Heidof cemetery.

Beamish at the helm

On 5 September 1942, while Gp Capt Charles Beamish DFC took over as station commander, the Bomber Wing passed to Wg Cdr J J Sutton and the Fighter Wing to Wg Cdr P G R Walker DSO DFC.

Among the most common reasons for the litany of accidents were pilot error; collision; engine failure; burst tyres and undercarriage collapses – although one Wellington, P9209, did manage to hit a tree but staggered back to base without crashing. This was flown by WO David North-Bomford, a staff pilot and Battle of Britain veteran; one of the many colourful characters to serve at the CGS. The son of an Earl, he held a commission in the pre-war RAF before resigning then re-joining as an NCO pilot on the outbreak of war. 'Bomber' – as he was known – was noted for his 'natty' line in richly-lined uniforms, sporting a large ginger handlebar moustache and was often seen on duty wearing exotic headgear such as a wide-brimmed Stetson or a jockey hat! On 6 July, 'Bomber', with air-gunner trainees on board, got into difficulty, this time in Wellington L7774 – another real 'oldie' – while on their way to the Wash range. Failure of a piston caused oil pressure to drop in the port engine and it caught fire. Unable to maintain height, North-Bomford could not make it back to the airfield so he force landed at Basses Farm, Wingland. He and the crew, some of whom were slightly injured, managed to scramble clear before the Wellington went up in flames and was completely burned out.

Here come the WAAFs

However, amid all this gloom, it would not have passed unnoticed to airmen on the station that the population rose substantially with the arrival in May 1942 of no less than two officers and 181 other ranks of the Women's Auxiliary Air Force (WAAF). In this contingent was Corporal (W) Olive Moule (later Mrs Olive Denis) who shared memories, both fond and sad, of Sutton Bridge during her service there in 1942/3.

At first she worked in the photographic section, helping to process "all those miles of cine-gun film", before transferring to the Bomber Wing with its Wellingtons and air gunners. Here, Olive was corporal in charge of a gun turret – one, though, which remained firmly fixed to the ground – an early example of a simulator. An air-gunner sat in this turret while Cpl Moule moved it randomly and manually through a set of levers and cams. While counteracting the motion of the turret, gunners 'fired' at a screen displaying cine-film images of attacking fighters. There was also sadness for Olive Moule at Sutton Bridge. While at CGS, she met and married a young air gunner who was attending one of the Gunnery Leader's courses. They married on 10 April 1943, but just one week later her husband was killed over Germany on what would have been his last operation before being posted as an instructor.

Six more fatalities were caused on 13 August 1943, when Spitfire P7530 and Wellington P9228 collided a few miles north-west of Lakenheath, halfway through a joint exercise. Even with the evidence of two survivors it was difficult to establish a cause but, in its conclusion, the enquiry cited a classic situation. It was felt that the Spitfire pilot, Flt Lt H C Bennett, misjudged the forward momentum of his aircraft on breakaway from his attack while the Wellington pilot, Flt Lt F M Shannon, was still changing his position during the attack. The Spitfire lost its port wing and spun in inverted and the Wellington crashed a few fields away in Stallode Fen.

At Command level there was always a continuing debate over the suitability of Sutton Bridge airfield for CGS. In February 1943, the RAF Inspector General reported: "its accommodation is restricted, insufficient and inconvenient and not of a type that lends itself to good appearance. The airfield is small, being only 500yd across east to west and liable to be out of action due to water-logging in wet weather. On the other hand, the nearby Ranges are excellent." The outcome was that, after a two-year sojourn at Sutton Bridge, with effect from 23 February 1944 the CGS moved to Catfoss in Yorkshire.

Formed at Weeton, Blackpool, No.8 School of Technical Training was formed on 21 May 1940 to undertake conversion courses for RAF Flight Mechanics and Flight Riggers. The school had a number of airframes at its disposal including this unidentified Wellington pictured on 2 December 1941. (*Aeroplane*)

Chapter 9

The High-Altitude Pathfinder Wimpys

In 1938, a question was posed to Vickers as to whether it was feasible to convert a Wellington to operate at altitudes between 35,000ft and 40,000ft, by using a pressurised cabin for the crew. Only Short and Fairey had experimented with pressure cabins before, for civilian projects, which meant that Vickers was basically working from a blank sheet of paper. Despite no large orders materialising, the project was successful and other manufacturer's aircraft would, in the future, benefit from Vickers' findings.

The high-altitude Wellington would be built in two versions, the Mk V (converted from Mk ICs) powered by Hercules engines and the Mk VI powered by Merlin 60 engines. The main feature of both aircraft was the re-modelled forward fuselage, which contained the pressurised cabin. The cabin was attached to the geodetic airframe by integral feet that were anchored to various nodal points. The pilot flew the aircraft from the upper section of the cabin through a small bubble canopy.

Designed to Specification B.23/29 and 17/40 the first Mk V, R3298, was fitted with a pair of Hercules III engines while the second aircraft, R3299, had a pair of more powerful Hercules VIIIs, with

One of 64 Mk Vs built was W5798, which is pictured during performance trials with the A&AEE out of Boscombe Down. The aircraft was SOC on 29 March 1943.

There is no doubting the position of the Wellington Mk V/Vis pressure cabin in this view during production. Note the modified front support members.

exhaust-driven superchargers. However, the required ceiling was never reached and attention turned to the Merlin-powered Mk VI instead.

Developed simultaneously with the Mk V, the Mk VI was powered by a pair of 1,600hp Rolls-Royce Merlin 60 engines fitted with a two-speed, two-stage supercharger designed for high-altitude flying. The Mk VI was produced fully equipped for high-altitude bombing and provision was made for a pilot, navigator, bomb-aimer and wireless operator within the pressurised cabin. Armament was planned to be a pressurised Fraser-Nash FN70 rear turret, mounting four .303in machine guns, but a FN20A was fitted at first, because the FN70 was still under development.

The first of just three Mk V prototypes, R3298, was first flown from Brooklands on 25 September 1940 direct to Blackpool, following the Luftwaffe attack that hit the Weybridge factory earlier in the month. Flight trials began on 21 October with a climb to 20,000ft, which had to be curtailed as the

Wellington Mk V and VI	
ENGINE	(V) Two Bristol Hercules VIII; (VI) Two Rolls-Royce Merlin 60
WINGSPAN	86ft 2in
LENGTH	(V) 64ft 7in; (VI) 61ft 9in
HEIGHT	17ft 5in
WING AREA	840sq ft
SERVICE CEILING	(V) 30,000ft; (VI) 40,000ft
RANGE	(VI) 1,590 miles with 4,500lb bomb load and 2,275 miles with 1,500lb load

The first Mk V, R3298, nearing completion at Foxwarren, Cobham.

pilot's canopy iced up. Further flights continued until 30,000ft was reached on 31 October, which was as high as any Mk V could climb, simply because the Hercules engines were out of their optimum performance zone.

The Mk VI was more successful, the first of 64 built, W5795, first flew in November 1941. The Merlin 60 engines were more suited to high-altitude work and the Mk VI was capable of reaching 40,000ft as requested by the Air Ministry.

It was hoped that the Mk VI could serve as a specialised pathfinder aircraft for Bomber Command and four aircraft did served with 109 Squadron at Tempsford and Stradishall between March and July 1942. However, the only really suitable aircraft for this task, which was already available was the Mosquito, which 109 Squadron converted to in December 1942.

Key dates	
25 September 1940	Mk V, R3298 first flight direct to Blackpool
November 1941	First flight of Mk VI, W5795
March 1942	Mk VI joins 109 Sqn at Tempsford
12 July 1942	Only loss, W5795 crashes near Derby
January 1943	Last Mk VI, DR528 delivered but SOC by March
11 November 1945	Last Mk VI, W5802 SOC after serving Rotol

WELLINGTON MK V, VI AND VA PRODUCTION

Mk V; Two converted from Mk IC and one from Mk VI contract; R3298 (ex-Mk IC; f/f 25 September 1940; Mkrs/A&EE/TFU/Bristols; SOC 5 March 1943); R3299 (ex-Mk IC; Mkrs/A&EE; to 3540M 16 January 1943); W5796* (A&EE; crashed 12 July 1942).

Mk VI (first batch); Including Mk V W5796, 21 Mk Vs were delivered between January and June 1942 by Vickers Weybridge to Contract 67578/40; W5796* (Bristols; SOC 5 March 1943), W5797 (R-R; to 3499M 17 January 1942); W5798 (A&EE; SOC 29 March 1943); W5799 (Mkrs; SOC 1 November 1943); W5800 (Mkrs/A&EE/RAE; SOC 24 June 1943); W5801 (109 Sqn; SOC 11 August 1943); W5802 (109Sqn/RAE; 5750M NTU; SOC 22 November 1945); W5803 (SOC 7 June 1942); W5804 (SOC 12 September 1943); W5805 (SOC 12 September 1943); W5806 (SOC 12 September 1943); W5807 (SOC 6 April 1943); W5808 (SOC June 1943); W5809 (SOC 19 July 1943); W5810 (SOC 9 June 1943); W5811 (SOC 9 June 1943); W5812 (SOC 28 May 1943); W5813 (12 September 1943); W5814 (SOC 19 July 1943); W5815 (SOC 31 July 1943).

Mk VI (second batch); 44 Mk VI & VIA (DR485-527) delivered between May 1942 and January 1943 by Vickers, Weybridge; DR471–473 (SOC 5 August 1944); DR474 (7 June 1944); DR475 (Rotol; SOC 11 July 1944); DR476 (SOC 1 June 1944); DR477 (SOC 7 June 1944); DR478–479 (SOC 1 June 1944); DR480** (Mkrs/TFU; SOC 1 March 1943); DR481 (109 Sqn; 3 April 1944); DR482*** (A&EE; SOC 30 June 1943); DR483 (SOC 6 April 1943); DR484 (A&EE; SOC 30 December 1943); DR485 (109 Sqn); DR486–491 (SOC 29 June 1943); DR492 (SOC 12 Sep 1943); DR493–497 (all SOC 6 Jul 1943); DR498–500 (all SOC 20 July 1943); DR502–504 and DR519–520 (all SOC 6 April 1943); DR521 (SOC 25 November 1943); DR522-523 (SOC 3 April 1943); DR525 (RAE; 15 July 1944); DR526 (SOC 16 November 1943); DR527 (SOC 31 October 1943); DR528 (SOC 1 March 1943); DR529–549 and DR566–600 all cancelled.

A view through the access door of the pressurised cabin of a Mk V showing the wireless operator's position on the left-hand side. The cabin was mounted so that it could expand and contract independently of the geodetic structure.

The crew compartment of the pressure cabin viewed from the rear access door. The pilot's seat was mounted on the shelf in the foreground while the navigator/bombers position was further forward. The pilot's head projected into a pressurised transparent dome which made landing particularly challenging in terms of visibility.

DR484 was one of four aircraft that served with 109 Squadron out of Tempsford, Bedfordshire, and Stradishall, West Sussex, between March and July 1942. The aircraft was also trialled by the A&AEE until it was SOC on 30 December 1943.

The prototype Wellington Mk V, R3298, which was flown north, away from the attentions of the Luftwaffe in September 1940. The aircraft, fitted with Hercules engines, could not quite reach the criteria set out by the Air Ministry.

LOSS AND INCIDENTS

*W5796. On 12 July 1942, the crew of W5796 were tasked with carrying out a performance climb to 35,000ft, followed by a level speed assessment with a light load. Witnesses saw the Wellington enter a dive at high speed from a high altitude before breaking up and hitting the ground over a wide area over Stanley, five miles north-east of Derby.

The most likely cause of the accident was the failure was a burst oil cooler which caused No.4 propeller blade on the starboard engine to detach and penetrated the pressure cabin, forward of the pilot's cockpit dome. The pilot, Sqn Ldr Cyril L F Colmore, of the High Altitude Flight, A&AEE was either injured or incapacitated, leading to total loss of control. Five crew in total were killed including the pilot; they were Plt Off Kenneth Radford (AG), Sgt Arthur J Smith (Air Observer), Sgt Ronald P Gillott (WOp/AG) and Mr C V Abbott (Flight Test Observer). Aircraft Category 5.

**DR480. On 16 October 1942, Plt Off R H A Williams of 'B' Flight, Performance Test Squadron, A&AEE was tasked with carrying out a general handling flight. On landing, the Wellington landed heavily. This combined with the uneven surface of the runway, caused the tailwheel assembly to collapse. Category 3 damage was caused with no injury to the crew.

***DR482. Sqn Ldr J W S Truran and Sgt F Stephenson (WOp/AG) of 'B' Flight, Performance Test Squadron, A&AEE were trialling M gear level speeds on 14 January 1943. On return to Boscombe Down, the pilot carried out too slow an approach and the subsequent heavy landing, on to a soft surface, caused the main starboard undercarriage and tailwheel to collapse. The aircraft nosed over causing Category 5 damage with no injury to the two crew.

Vickers Wellington Mk VI, DR484, pictured at Brooklands, complete with a production-type nose. Installed with Type 423 bomb gear, the aircraft was the second to be capable of dropping a 4,000lb bomb. Note the lack of rear turret and Avro Lancaster-type engine cowlings.

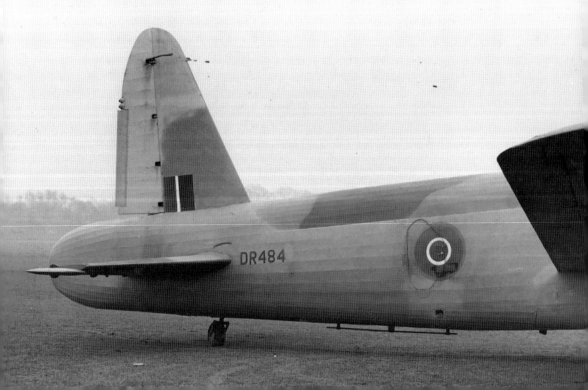

The starboard Rolls-Royce Merlin 60 of a Wellington Mk VI with the main radiator, flanked by the oil and intercooler radiators.

Chapter 10

Wellington Ops in Italy

The Mediterranean Allied Air Force (MAAF) had a sub-division known as the Mediterranean Allied Strategic Air Force (MASAF) of which the RAF's 205 Group was a component. In Italy, strategic control of 205 Group was exercised by the US 15th Air Force; the only time that an RAF formation was subject to control by a foreign air force. Within 205 Group were five RAF Wings, one of which was 236 Wing. This wing comprised 40 and 104 Squadrons, which were co-located at an airfield known as Foggia Main – also home to 205 Group HQ. No.205 Group was known affectionately as the 'Alamein to the Alps Group', indicating the widespread operational area covered by the Group during World War Two. From 1943 onwards it operated from bases in North Africa and then, after the invasion of Italy, from airfields on the Plain of Foggia, where its efforts were intended to complement and extend those of its 'big brother', Bomber Command. However, while the purposes and effectiveness were similar, the scale and scope of MAAF operations were quite different from those of its UK counterpart. Where Bomber Command could number its aircraft in thousands, the more modest scale of 205 Group is best illustrated by a remark made by an intelligence officer during one pre-operation briefing. After the usual discourse on target defences, this chap announced: "Bomber Command has recently lost 70 aircraft in a

raid on a nearby target," then after a pause continued, "We shall not lose 70 aircraft tonight, gentlemen – we are only sending out 56!"

To put this into perspective, an analysis of 205 Group operational records between February 1944 and end of April 1945 shows an average of 63 aircraft were despatched on bombing operations (as opposed to leaflet raids) on 283 out of a possible 430 nights. It was only on relatively few occasions that the number despatched exceeded 100 but during this same period the Group lost 215 aircraft in action.

Doddy

Sgt Derek Dodimead (known as 'Doddy') joined 104 Squadron on 10 March 1944 as navigator in Sgt Fred Williams's crew, when the aircraft operated by the two RAF squadrons at Foggia Main was the Wellington Mk X. For the crews, most of the navigation aids in use by Bomber Command were non-existent in Italy (for example, Gee, Oboe, H2S) and 205 Group navigators worked by much the same means as they had learned in their early basic training – map reading, dead reckoning, drift-sights, some radio direction-finding (DF) and astro-shots – but the reputation of 205 Group for 'spot on' delivery became legendary. Bad weather, icing and topographical features such as the Alps (up to 15,000ft), Dolomites, Dinaric Alps, Balkan and Carpathian Mountains (up to 9,000ft) were particular hazards – along with the usual danger from flak and night fighters.

The high-altitude Wellington Mk VI and Mk V stemmed from a 1938 Air Ministry requirement calling for a civilian aircraft capable of flying higher than normal to avoid poor weather at lower altitudes. The requirement was extended to a bomber that could potentially fly so high it would be immune from flak and fighters. (Via Martyn Chorlton)

In the first half of April 1944, 104 Squadron flew night operations to bomb the Macchi aircraft factory at Varese east of Lake Maggiore, railway yards at Leghorn, port installations at Porto San Stefano, armament factories and the Tokol airfield in Budapest, railways and industry in Bucharest and an operation to an important marshalling yard at Turnu-Severin just inside the Romanian border. They were also called upon on 8 April to send three Wellingtons to join some more from 40 Squadron and aircraft from the 15th Air Force in supporting Marshal Tito's Partisans encircling a substantial German garrison in the town of Niksic, in the mountains of Yugoslavia [now Serbia].

First operational sortie

When conditions allowed, rookie crews were eased into things by having the pilot and navigator go off separately as supernumeraries with an experienced crew who would 'show them the ropes'. Thus, Sgt Fred Williams flew his first operational sortie to Leghorn on the night of 16–17 April as 'second dickey' pilot in Sgt Clifford's aircraft, LN841, to watch how this experienced pilot carried out an 'op'.

Sgt Dodimead was scheduled to fly his own first operation the following night (17–18 April) as 'second navigator' in Fg Off Robert Avery's crew – but it was not to be! The target, revealed as the railway marshalling yards at Plovdiv, was a major transport hub 500 miles east of Foggia in southern Bulgaria and the raid would involve 43 aircraft drawn from 104 and 40 Squadrons from Foggia Main together with two squadrons from another airfield. As the time for take-off approached, Avery's aircraft, number four in the second wave, was trundling along the taxiway in a long queue of bombers heading towards the threshold. He watched as, just after 20:00hrs, five Wellingtons from 104 thundered at two-minute intervals down the runway. Next aircraft to go was 'K' from 40 Squadron. It lined up, the pilot 'opened the taps' and off it went – but things went dreadfully wrong. 'K' crashed during take-off, caught fire, collided with and set fire to two other aircraft. Everyone in aeroplanes and on the ground realised that the burning 'K' had a 4,000lb 'Cookie' (or 'Blockbuster') bomb that was going to explode at any minute.

Ops were back on for the night of 19–20 April and this time all went well for Doddy's first 'op', made with Fg Off Avery in Wellington Mk X, JM512. Destination for this milestone trip was Piombino, a port on the Tuscany coast opposite the island of Elba; a 600-mile round trip.

No. 205 Group was busy that night, despatching 83 aircraft to a variety of targets, 24 to Porto San Stefano, 23 to Leghorn harbour, 20 to Piombino, seven to Genoa harbour and nine to Plovdiv (Bulgaria) railyards. All bar one returned safely. Twelve Wellingtons from 104 Squadron were detailed for this

104 Squadron official group photograph while the unit was still operating the Wellington Mk II and before its relocation from North Africa to Southern Italy.

A 104 Squadron Wellington prepares to receive delivery of a full load of 500lb bombs.

raid, in three waves of four aircraft each. Fg Off Avery was in the second wave and took off at 23:30hrs. Target for the Wellington's load of six 500lb and four 250lb bombs was the harbour installation and the operation itself was classed as an 'harassing raid'. Visibility was good all the way to the target and remained so for the first two waves of aircraft over the port. The third and final wave found cloud had rolled in, covering the aiming point and the aircraft bombed by dead reckoning. All aircraft encountered fairly accurate heavy and light flak in the target area but there were no casualties. Doddy's bomb-aimer

'Flak Happy Harry', the 104 Squadron Wellington of Sgt Doug Skinner and crew at Foggia in February 1945. (S J Sterrett)

dropped a flare to illuminate the target then released all his bombs as a single stick. Explosions from these were seen inland of the South Mole and halfway through their stick the aiming point was lit up by a large white flash which seemed to indicate something vital had been hit. The aircraft landed back at Foggia Main at 04:05hrs. Fred Williams was also airborne as second dickey again with Sgt Clifford in LN841, whose bombs were dropped on the harbour mole.

Recalls and 'second dickey'

Piombino was on the cards for the 20–21 April but after seven aircraft had taken off, Group HQ issued a 'recall', due to bad weather, before any of them reached the target. Next night, the weather improved, so Piombino port and marshalling yard was back on again and at Foggia Main, 13 aircraft were made ready. This time just three Wellingtons managed to get airborne before the next two aircraft each suffered a burst tyre during take-off and crashed, fortunately without casualties. The first managed to exit the runway but the second did not and it lay wrecked in the middle of the runway, preventing any more take-offs. The three aircraft that had become airborne located their target in hazy conditions and dropped their bombs before having to land at another airfield. Next day operations were cancelled while the runway was cleared up once more. Fred Williams went on another trip to Leghorn as 'second dickey' with WO T T C Stephens' crew on 23–24 April, one of 91 aircraft on ops that night, but then the weather took a turn for the worse and continual torrential downpours over the next three days flooded the runway and put it out of action again. Leghorn was attacked on 29–30 April but due to thick cloud cover no one actually found the target. Only a few unloaded their bombs on targets of opportunity while others jettisoned their bombs and several aircraft were scattered around different airfields for their return landings.

Flt Sgt Ivor Courtney was tasked to fly with Fred Williams in LP181 on that evening's 'op', acting as a supernumerary but on hand to give Fred the benefit of his experience.

Flt Sgt Courtney had been 'in the wars' before Doddy arrived at Foggia. During the return leg of an 'op' to bomb an aircraft factory at Steyr in Austria on 24–25 February foul weather conditions set in and with radio failure, he and his crew were unable to locate their base. After a fruitless search and eight and a half hours in the air, their aircraft finally ran out of fuel. At 02:50hrs, just before the last dregs of petrol were used up, Flt Sgt Courtney gave the order to bale out. Several of the crew, including Courtney, were slightly injured upon landing and the Wellington, ME876, crashed in the vicinity of Altamura, near Bari, about 150 miles south of Foggia.

A Wimpy takes off.

The trip scheduled for 4–5 May would be Courtney's first since his mis-hap. From 205 Group, 70 aircraft, including eight from 104 Squadron, were detailed to attack the Rakos railway marshalling yard at Budapest and the Wellingtons began to roll down Foggia Main's runway at 21:40hrs. Flt Sgt Courtney in LP181 with Sgts Williams, Dodimead, Viner, Reikie and Veasey, plus six 500lb; three 250lb and a batch of nickels on board, took off at 21:53hrs on what would be a six-hour round trip. The target was due to be marked by Halifax bombers from the group's 614 Squadron but the red target illuminators (TIs) went down late and although quite visible, they seemed to be very spread out. These TIs also dazzled the bomb-aimer so Fred Williams held the run-up heading and the bomb load was released in the general target area. Flak was moderate and not very accurate with the crews reporting they had seen about 35 guns, 15 searchlight batteries and at least one Junkers Ju88 night-fighter in the vicinity. One aircraft failed to find the target and dropped its bombs on a 'target of opportunity' and the loss was that of Fg Off Robert Avery's aircraft with all on board.

Sgt Williams and his crew had to wait nearly a week before they did a trip entirely on their own. In the meantime, the squadron continued to mount operations almost every night. On 5–6 May, ten aircraft went to the Steaua-Romana refinery and marshalling yard at Campina, near Ploieşti in Romania. On 6–7 May, 13 bombed Bucharest; the following night, 12 aircraft attacked a bridge at Filiaşi in southwest Romania; and on 9–10 May five aircraft bombed Genoa in northern Italy. These were long distances for the Wellington but very typical of the operations being mounted by the squadrons of 205 Group.

Supporting the Maquis

Further evidence of the versatility of 205 Group's squadrons came on 9–10 May, when another seven aircraft from 104 Squadron were despatched, as part of a 24-strong force, in support of a top-secret operation by the French Maquis near the town of Portes-les-Valences on the river Rhone, north of Avignon. Intelligence rumours had it that the Germans were storing hundreds of Henschel Hs293 radio-controlled, anti-ship glide-bombs in a factory at this location. Having been used – although not very successfully – at Salerno and Anzio, these 'stand-off' guided weapons posed a potentially serious threat to any amphibious landings and, most worryingly, for those planned for the imminent D-Day. The Allies, therefore, were desperate to get hold of one of these weapons in order to examine its radio-guidance system and come up with effective counter-measures. Under cover of darkness and a diversionary bombing raid on a railway yard about a mile away, the French Resistance fighters, acting in conjunction with Allied intelligence agents, intended to break into the factory and steal a bomb. To assist them, 205 Group laid on a bombing raid, with the first wave having the primary objective of breaching the perimeter walls to open up access to the factory for the Maquis. The second wave, 15 minutes later, would be a diversionary raid directed at the marshalling yard in Porte-lès-Valences, about a mile from the factory. The plan was daring but the Maquis was ready.

This target was at extreme range for the Wellington so the four squadrons involved, including 104 and 40 at Foggia Main, were each ordered to send their aircraft contribution to this operation to a forward-landing ground at Cagliari, on Sardinia. Departure for this three-and-a-half hour trip from Foggia was 12:20hrs on 9 May. Then, bombed-up and re-fuelled, the seven 104 Squadron Wellingtons, part of the first wave, took-off for Portes-lès-Valences at intervals between 23:40hrs and 00:45hrs. Crossing the French coast near Cannes, the weather deteriorated rapidly and it was now that the carefully co-ordinated plan was ruined.

Fg Off R A Billen in LM389, passed Cap d'Antibes by dead reckoning and in the vicinity of Montélimar, experienced severe icing at 12,000ft, which cracked and damaged the astrodome. Unsure of his position; unable to maintain altitude and with one magneto playing up, he decided to jettison his bombs on 'safe' and turn back to Sardinia, which he reached after five hours in the air. Fg Off F A Ashbaugh in ME871, Fg Off C F J Watts in LN430 (the latter with a 4,000lb 'cookie') and Flt Sgt E J Holmes in LP131 all experienced similar icing and navigational difficulties and they, too, reluctantly turned back. Flt Sgt R J Smith in LP122 located the distinctive bend in the river near the target and believed he had dropped his bombs north of the railway yard in the vicinity of the factory. WO KO Harrison in LN857 also thought he had put his bombs down near the factory. Sqn Ldr LW Richards who, in LN760, was first away from Cagliari at 23:40hrs, spotted some lights in the target area and attempted several bombing runs but each time the target became obscured by cloud. In the foul weather and with ice making it difficult to coax his aircraft to climb, he finally decided to abort and dropped his 4,000lb 'cookie' at a safe distance. Turning for home, he ran into a severe electrical storm and a build-up of static caused an explosion in the aircraft that tore holes in the fuselage and astrodome and burned some fabric from the wing tips. Rather than try to find Cagliari, Sqn Ldr Richards decided to head directly for Foggia where he landed safely at 07:05hrs – a trip of seven and a half hours. The remaining six aircraft all made it to Cagliari then re-positioned back to Foggia later that same day.

Fifteen minutes later, in clearer weather, the second wave arrived over the railway yards and bombed successfully. However, because the factory walls had not been breached by the first wave, the Maquis fighters could not gain access and had to melt away into the hills without the missile.

Portoferraio

On 11–12 May, a 'harassing attack' was made by 12 aircraft, including Fred Williams in MF137, against Portoferraio on the Isle of Elba. Their bombs were aimed at a harbour mole but no results were observed and they landed back at 04:03hrs. The squadron returned to the same target the following night, with 11 aircraft, in a further effort to disrupt the enemy from unloading stores at the port. This time two aircraft were lost; one with the loss of three of the crew while the other, captained by CO Wg Cdr Turner DFC, was obliged to crash land near Naples en route to the target, but with the crew all safe. The squadron carried out successful operations against German communications targets on 13–14 May, to the marshalling yard at Orvieto and a railway bridge at Fornovo di Taro while another rail bridge at Tagliamento was hit the following night. After mounting ops every night for seven days, the squadron was stood down on the 15th – but only for one day before it sent eight aircraft to harass the enemy again in Portoferraio.

Next day, the weather turned sour and continual heavy thunderstorms flooded the runway, stopping all ops until 20–21 May when nine aircraft raided the port of Piombino without opposition or loss.

104 Squadron officer group in front of a Wellington Mk II, which the unit operated from March 1941 to August 1943 when the Mk X took over until February 1945.

Showing how busy the Foggia airfield complex was, ground collisions were not uncommon; on this occasion the victim was 205 Group Wellington Mk X after an encounter with a USAAF P-47 on 27 December 1943.

Doddy's crew was back on ops on 22–23 May, one of ten Wellingtons from the squadron despatched to bomb a strategic road from Rome to Cassino at Valmontone, 20 miles south of Rome. Eight aircraft from 104 Squadron were despatched on 25–26 May to attack roads around Viterbo, a large town 40 miles north of Rome. This was a joint day/night operation with the 15th Air Force, which later reported that it believed more than 1,000 enemy vehicles were destroyed.

Next night, 26–27 May, another attack was launched against road and rail communications in the Viterbo district. No.104 sent eight aircraft to Viterbo, but Sgt Williams and his crew were selected for a special solo Nickel raid over the districts of Arad and Timişoara in eastern Romania, some 400 miles east of Foggia. All went well as they crossed the Aegean Sea, but climbing into Yugoslavia over the Dinaric Alps they ran into some foul weather. For an hour, Fred Williams tried time and again to climb above the cloud, which was solid up to at least 13,000ft but due to severe icing up to 12,000ft he had a job to coax Wellington MF137 over the mountains and after much climbing and diving, he decided to call it off and return to base.

No.104's night campaign continued with Viterbo again bombed by ten aircraft on 27–28 May, while there was a mixed set of targets laid on for the squadron on the following night. One aircraft, that of Sgt D A Nevill, managed to complete the previously aborted Nickel raid on Arad and Timisoara in Romania, while eight aircraft plastered port installations at San Stephano and three aircraft hauled 4,000lb 'cookies' to Colle Isarco, deep among the mountainous Alpine valleys, 25 miles south of Innsbruck. The latter objective was to drop the cookies and create a landslide on the mountain sides that would block the important railway running through the Brenner Pass. One of these three Wellingtons, flown by

A 104 Squadron Wellington Mk X warms through its two 1,675hp Bristol Hercules VI/XVI 14-cylinder two-row radial engines.

Plt Off P J T Pile, suffered engine trouble on the way north. The port engine only gave half power and in view of the approaching mountainous terrain he decided to turn back. Later, the engine began to cut out and the propeller was feathered. In order to maintain altitude Pile's crew began throwing out flares, guns and ammunition to lighten the load and he was able to land safely at Biferno/Campomarino airfield. Finding the target valley was quite a navigational challenge as all the valleys seemed to look alike and the separate Target Illuminator bombers had failed to find the target in darkness. However, both crews were confident they were at the correct position when the two cookies were dropped and both bombs were seen to detonate.

Sgt Williams was next on ops on the night of 30–31 May when the squadron sent nine aircraft to attack a road running through Subiaco, 25 miles east of Rome. Airborne in MF137 at 22:18hrs, it was a short trip and the hefty load of nine 500lb and three 250lb bombs, with the usual bundles of Nickels for afters, was laid on the road system around the village in two sticks and they were back at Foggia by 00:33hrs. This trip turned out to be his – and his crew's – last wartime flight in a Wellington bomber. They were about to be posted away from Foggia Main to convert to the B-24 Liberator bomber, which was being rolled out to MAAF squadrons in the Italian theatre.

Before Wellington Mk III Z1572 arrived at 419 (Moose) Squadron, the fortunate bomber had already been in action with 115 and 75 (NZ) Squadrons. The Wellington went on to also serve 427 (Lion) Squadron and finally 16 OTU without incident until April 1945. (Charles E brown via *Aeroplane*)

Chapter 11

Wimpy Pick-up

'We settled into a steady climb at maximum wheels-down speed to get just enough height to skim over the Taza Pass.' (*Aeroplane*)

When a Wimpy, bound for Fez, Morocco, lost its way and force-landed in a mountain valley, Air Marshal Tony Dudgeon volunteered to go and retrieve it. This is his story.

When the disembarkation code-named 'Torch' took place in Morocco and Algeria, it opened up tremendous savings for moving aircraft into the Middle East war theatre. Up until 1942 there was only one access route, 5,000 miles in crates by sea to the African Gold Coast. After being assembled they were flown from Takoradi via Accra, Lagos, and then northwards and eastwards over largely featureless and radio-less country to Khartoum. From there they flew north along the Nile valley to Cairo and the war. After *Torch*, it would be easy in comparison. The long-range aircraft such as the Wellingtons and Beauforts would be delivered direct to the theatre by their own posted crews right on to the doorstep, as it were. I became partly responsible for their safe arrival in Morocco, working from an airstrip near Fez. It was not always as easy as it looked.

There were many problems. One of them was that newly fledged crews, hastily trained in wartime, were stressed by an overnight, overwater, flight of nine to ten hours. They found themselves, in the early light, over unfamiliar topography, with different edition maps. They couldn't assimilate that a brown earth strip, graded on farmland, with a number of tents, constituted a terminal airfield. Our radio D/F equipment was strictly elementary and the wireless operators, both in the air and on the ground, were also inexperienced. So crews often became utterly lost.

Irrevocably lost and short of fuel

Thus it was that, in gin clear weather, a Wellington crew sailed straight over Fez one morning. We called them on the radio and fired Very lights. They went serenely past. Fifty miles farther on they had to climb to 6,000ft to cross the Taza pass in the Atlas Mountains. Having got to the other side and cast around a bit, they decided they were both irrevocably lost and short of fuel and they were correct on both counts. They did not fly down to the plains but picked a fairly small field on the sloping hillside of a narrow valley at about 5,000ft. They very sensibly landed uphill and, apart from swinging and collapsing one undercarriage leg at the end, emerged unscathed. They then walked down the valley in the balmy sunshine until they were found and brought in.

Having disposed of the crew, the next question was what we could do about the aircraft. COs of Ferry Wings were allowed to delay any aircraft if by so doing they could improve the overall flow. This was fairly liberally interpreted. For example, my friend 'Ricky' Rixson, running the Khartoum Wing, needed range and radio over the deserts. He therefore had his own Blenheim Mk V 'Bisley' with the turret and armour-plate removed clandestinely by the groundcrew. This lightening, by well over two tons, made the beastly Bisley into a very fast, pleasant and stable aircraft, locally christened a 'Wisley'. For me, I had my own private Hurricane with no armament. I took it to have a look at the Wellington.

How that solitary grassy field came to be there I had no idea. There were forests all round, no access roads and no apparent signs of habitation. There were a few tracks up, which one might get a jeep or a truck with four-wheel drive and a low-ratio gear box. A transporter was totally out of the question. One thing was certain; she would never come out on the ground. She sat drunkenly on one wing and looked as if she would never fly again either. She seemed destined to rot on the hillside, being gradually pilfered by the Moroccans until nothing remained but the spars, engines and other pieces, which were too heavy to carry away. wartime scrap.

Could a Wimpy accelerate downhill?

Being mechanically minded by nature and training the waste of machinery made with skill and pride gives me something akin to physical pain. Could she be flown out if lightened, I wondered? After all, it had been landed, with little apparent damage. How long was that field? How much space was there between its edge and the far side of the valley? Could a Wimpy accelerate down the hill, be coaxed off and then dive to pick up speed for a turn before reaching the opposite hillside?

I flew slowly parallel to the side of the valley and turned, flaps extended, to pass low over the Wellington and pointed across the field. The downslope was steeper than I had imagined; good. I went over the trees at the far end and nosed downhill, at the same throttle setting, to gather speed and began a gentle turn. The far side of the valley approached much too fast and I had to pile on the coal to climb out and away. Another go, with slightly less loss of height and a little tighter turn gave me a safer and potentially possible escape.

Several things were done over the next few days. The engineers and I went up in a jeep for a ground recce. They reckoned they could lift the aircraft up and jury-rig the undercarriage into a locked-down

37 Squadron, Wellington Mk X HE764 after a wheels-up landing at night following an engine failure at Hergla, Tunisia, on 23 July 1943; this bomber never flew again.

position. The damage to the rest of the aircraft appeared minimal, patchable and acceptable. A new prop could and would be fitted and, as the undercarriage collapse occurred at very low speed, shock-loading damage to the engine was unlikely. I paced out the possible take-off runs. The longest, about 600yds, faced most uncomfortably towards the hillside and there was some soft earth under the grass. The one that faced almost down the valley had a steep slope down and the hardest earth but it was only 400yd long. I compromised on 500yd and an acceptable turn between the two. I marked the trees to be felled at the far end to give me a 50yd-gap to fly through.

Lightening the load

It took the engineers a week to do their work. It was slow going as every bit of equipment had to go up in a jeep and big items had to be left behind. In the process they removed everything that was not nailed down aboard the aircraft and brought as much of it down the valley as the jeep could carry. That included all the radio and radar and even the navigator's desk. All the tanks were checked and drained except the two nacelle tanks. These had enough in them for one hour's cruising.

Meanwhile, as I could neither ask nor authorise anyone else to do the job, I set about learning how Wellingtons were flown. I enlisted the help of a Flying Officer from the delivery flow. He was a little man; dark, brown-eyed with a scrubby moustache. He had a habit of puffing out his cheeks while thinking. I believe he was rather pleased at being treated as the fount of knowledge for a senior officer who seemed to be somewhat moronic. A Wing Commander, no less, who in addition to wanting the take-off and landing drills dozens of times, kept asking questions on such unlikely things as the stall characteristics and slow-speed flying; which wing usually dropped first, and how effective were the ailerons at low speeds? What, if one wanted to get her off quickly, were the wrinkles about getting airborne; would he slam the flaps down? When – at the last moment? How far down? And so on. To most of these esoteric queries I got no answer. As he puffed out his cheeks, I felt he had trouble not tapping his forehead with one finger and slowly shaking his head. Poor fellow, I gave him no reasons as I did not want 'clever' invented answers; I wanted, and got, the sum total of his actual knowledge.

Finally, when the plumbers gave their thumbs-up, the day was perfect. High stratus to keep off the sun, cool air and little wind. I had a 45-minute flight plan. With the full run-up and take-off at full chat I would have little fuel in hand but to take more fuel would reduce the acceleration and that was a killer risk; I preferred to chance running dry on the way home. I entreated Flying Control to watch keenly for a westbound Wimpy with wheels down, which made no radio calls; to give him a green light because he was coming right in. Then off on the 100-mile jeep ride into the mountains.

Not all Wimpys could be flown out after a forced landing, this example will now be picked clean of all useful components and scrapped.

Throttles wide open!

Having done my pre-flight checks, I ran up both engines, which kindly delivered maximum revs with minimum mag drops. I was alarmed at how much the airframe vibrated and flexed; it felt as if it would fall to bits. I had been assured that this was normal. I waved away the chocks and opened up slowly against full brakes. As they began to slip I shoved the throttles wide open and let her go. Full stick forward to get the tail up to what I estimated was minimum drag attitude as soon as possible. Acceleration seemed to be OK but I had nothing really to judge it by. Nevertheless, I felt we were trundling down the hill impossibly slowly. The gap in the trees at the end, at least a couple of wing-spans wide, appeared to get smaller and smaller the closer and faster I got but I had passed the point of no return in the first ten seconds. I did not look at the airspeed indicator, which could only frighten me and do no good; she would, or she wouldn't, make it. I concentrated on the minuscule gap in the trees. Why hadn't we cut it wider? Twenty or 30 yards before the field's end I selected 15 degrees of flap and eased back on the stick. Miraculously, the trees missed the wing tips. Prickles were running up my spine.

She came off, but felt horribly sloppy. I realised I had been holding my breath. I eased the nose down all I dared and went gingerly into my turn. Admittedly we came scarily close to the far side of the valley but by then the speed was rising and I was even able to start holding height. All was well. I waggled my wings slightly as a 'Thank you' to the engineers behind me. We settled into a steady climb at maximum wheels-down speed to get just enough height to skim over the Taza Pass. That done, I nosed down thankfully and throttled back for the 50-mile drive home.

The boys in Flying Control must have had the field glasses out; I got a green Very light while I was still miles away.

Next day, I was on the telephone to the CO of the Maintenance Unit. He was, to me, just a disembodied voice whose owner I had not seen 'Well...' he said doubtfully, 'we can't leave it on your airfield. You'll have to arrange to fly her in here, wheels down all the way. Our trouble is that although we are assembling Spits and Hurricanes, we haven't got the equipment and jigs for a full-scale check-out on a Wimpy. And, after a crash landing, we can't let it go to a squadron without that. Of course, we can cannibalise a bit from what your chaps haven't removed already but, in effect, it'll just be scrapped.

On the Station we debated for a while as to whether we needed a junked Wellington as our private transport and communications aircraft but proper repair of the collapsed undercarriage leg was beyond the Station's capacity. Regretfully, we flew her in, wheels down, to the MU. My plumbers, whose stalwart and innovative work in a mountain field had made recovery possible, were quite acid about the disappointing ending to my first solo on type.

Hundreds of Wimpys were ferried to the Middle Eastern theatre during World War Two, the vast majority of them, including Wellington Mk II, Z8624 'U' of 205 Group with 52 operations' symbols on the nose, gave long and loyal service.

The RNZAF placed an order for 30 Wellington Mk Is in 1938, establishing new airfields at Whenuapai and Ohakea in New Zealand for their operation. The first 18 had been delivered just before the outbreak of the war, but in August 1939, they were loaned, complete with RNZAF aircrew, to the RAF. Prior to this, the New Zealand Flight was

formed on 1 June 1939 and on 4 April 1940 this became the nucleus for 75 (NZ) Squadron. This is a view inside the cockpit of one of the RNZAF's first Wellingtons NZ400, re-serialled L4311. The aircraft served with the NZ Flt, CGS and BAS, before becoming an instructional airframe in April 1942. Note the early dual controls. (*Aeroplane*)

Chapter 12

Post-War Wimpy Trainers

T he most prolific mark of Wellington built was the Mk X, the last example, RP590, rolling off the production line in October 1945. This was not, however, the end of the road for the Wimpy and the fact that the Mk X was structurally stronger than its predecessors made it an ideal candidate for modification and continued service. The engines were also considerably more efficient than earlier machines, the Hercules VI or XVI featuring carburettors with automatic mixture control, which improved performance no end.

The first Wellington 'flying classroom' was a conversion of the GR Mk XI, which was used to train Mosquito night-fighter crews. Re-designated as the Mk XVII (Type 487), the aircraft featured a modified nose, which contained an SCR-720 AI radome instead of the front turret. The Mk XVIII (Type 490) followed, with the same modifications as the Mk XVII, plus the provision for four pupils and an instructor. In total, 80 Mk XVIIIs were built, all at Blackpool.

Wellington T.10, MF628, during a cameo appearance in the classic war film *The Dambusters*, filmed in 1954. The scene shows Barnes Wallis (Michael Redgrave) leaving his personal transport to be greeted by a saluting Wg Cdr Guy Gibson (Richard Todd). (*Aeroplane*)

The first Wellington to receive a post-war conversion to a more passive role was a modification of the Mk X to a basic trainer. Designated the Mk XIX (T.19), work included the removal and fairing over of the front turret, while the rear turret remained but with both guns and hydraulics taken out. With no indication that dual controls were installed, the Wellington MK XIX was presented in silver finish, complete with yellow training bands. The RAF planned to convert 24 Mk Xs to Mk XIX standard and the work was to have been carried out at 24 MU at Stoke Heath. However, only half a dozen were ever converted and these only gave limited service before being placed into storage and later scrapped.

The final Wimpy

The final and most successful post-war conversion of the Wellington was the transformation of the Mk X into the T.10. The result was a most efficient navigation trainer, very similar to the T.19 but with the conversion work contracted out to Boulton Paul at Wolverhampton. The company carried out 270 conversions between January 1946 and March 1952, which involved a complete strip down, overhaul and re-covering of the aircraft before the key features were installed. These were the fitment of dual controls and a reconfiguration internally, so that a new navigator's station was positioned behind the main spar with enough space for two navigators and an instructor. A second GEE unit was also installed, additional aerials for the extra navigational aids, Lockheed hydraulic pumps and horn-balanced rudders. Just like the T.19s they all entered service with an overall silver finish and yellow bands from 1946.

The T.10 saw service with 1 Air Navigation School (ANS) at Topcliffe and Hullavington, 2 ANS at Bishop's Court and Middleton St George, 5 ANS at Topcliffe, 6 ANS at Lichfield, 7 ANS (re-designated 2 ANS) at Bishop's Court and 10 ANS (disbanded into 1 and 2 ANS March 1948). The T.10 also served 201 Advanced Flying School (AFS) at Swinderby and 202 AFS at Finningley, the former being one of the last bastions when the type was finally replaced by the Varsity T.1 and the Valetta T.3. The last T.10 to be retired in RAF service was LP806 by 1 ANS in March 1953.

Wellington T.10 carried out the final Wimpy flight on 24 January 1955 when Flt Sgt 'Herbie' Marshall (Pilot) and Jim C Pickersgill (Flight Engineer) delivered the aircraft to Wisley for preservation. (Via Martyn Chorlton)

Lone survivor

It was thanks to longevity of the Wellington T.10 that this country enjoyed one sole survivor until 1985, when the RAF Museum's aircraft, serialled MF628, was joined by the famous Mk IA, N2980, raised from the depths of Loch Ness in 1985 and now on display at the Brooklands Museum, Weybridge. MF628, ordered as a Mk X in May 1942, first flew in May 1944 and, after a brief foray with 69 Squadron, was placed in storage until selected for conversion to a T.10 in early 1948. MF628 joined 1 ANS, serving until October 1952 when the first Varsity T.1s began to arrive. Flown to 19 MU at St Athan, the aircraft was kept airworthy, taking part in the Royal Aeronautical Society's '50 years of Aviation' Garden Party at Hatfield in June 1953 and Battle of Britain displays at Aston Down and St Athan, before being placed into storage.

In April 1954, MF628 took part in the film *The Dambusters*, initially being hired for just three days, but the Wellington remained much longer. MF628 was used as a camera ship throughout the film, the aircraft also making a couple of cameos, including a brief appearance in one of the take-off scenes. Grounded in October 1954, the aircraft was sold to Vickers on 24 January 1955 and flown to Wisley from St Athan by Flt Sgt 'Herbie' Marshall the same day. Filmed en route by an Airspeed Oxford, this was the last flight of a Vickers Wellington.

Under RAF Hendon charge from 1957, the aircraft was moved several times before settling back at the RAF Museum in 1971. In 1981, MF628 was restored back to its original Mk X configuration and from 1983 was moved to the Bomber Command Hall until 2010 when it was dismantled for long-term full restoration at RAF Cosford.

The bulbous nose of this Wimpy gives it away as the Mk XVIII with a SCR720 AI radome in place of the front turret. (Via Martyn Chorlton)

MF628 being exhibited at the RAF 50th Anniversary Royal Review at RAF Abingdon in June 1968. (Mike Hooks)

Vickers Warwick ASR.1, HF944 sporting invasion stripes indicating that the aircraft would have been operating with 282 Squadron from Davidstow Moor, Cornwall, at the time. The squadron disbanded in July 1945 but HF944 is recorded as crashing into trees at Silloth, Cumbria, after a failed overshoot on 8 July 1946. (Via Martyn Chorlton)

Chapter 13

Overshadowed Younger Sibling

Warwick (B.1/95), B Mk I and B Mk II

T he Warwick started out as a heavy bomber version of the Wellington, an aircraft it had a great deal in common with, such as the geodetic airframe. Unfortunately, the Warwick, as a bomber, would prove unsuccessful because, from the outset, the Vickers designers were forced into using an engine that would not achieve even modest performance figures demanded by the specification.

Designed to Specification B.1/35, the Vickers Type 284 was tendered as a heavy bomber, of which the Air Ministry had requested should be capable of carrying 2,000lb of bombs over a distance of 2,000 miles at a cruising speed of no less than 195mph at 15,000ft. Another demand was that the wingspan should not be greater than 100ft so that it could be easily moved in and out of the standard RAF hangars of the day.

The first production Warwick B Mk I, BV214, one of just 16 built, was first flown in April 1942. The aircraft was delivered to the A&EE for trials but crashed on 26 August 1942 when a large section of wing fabric was lost. (Via Martyn Chorlton)

The Vickers tender stated that the aircraft should be powered by the Bristol Hercules, which would have exceeded the above figures. However, as time rolled by, the Vickers tender was compared to the later Specification P.13/36, which the Avro Manchester had been tendered, resulting in the Warwick prototype being fitted with the under-developed Rolls-Royce Vulture or the Napier Sabre. As a result, two prototypes were ordered under the original B.1/35 and modified to include one aircraft powered by the Vulture and the other, the Napier.

The first Vulture-powered Warwick prototype, serialled K8178, was first flown by Mutt Summers out of Brooklands on 13 August 1939. The Rolls-Royce engine was already suffering from a variety of problems and, as a result, the number of restrictions placed upon it, made K8178 virtually useless from a developmental point of view. Attention was then turned to the second prototype, L9704, which by then, was engine-less because all Napier engine production had been diverted solely to the Hawker Typhoon.

This gave Vickers the opportunity to fit the engine that they really wanted, the Bristol Centaurus 18-cylinder sleeve-vale radial and, with this powerplant, L9704 first flew on 5 April 1940. By then though, all focus was being placed on producing the four-engined heavies, which led Vickers to look at another alternative engine for the Warwick. L9704 was then converted with a pair of Pratt & Whitney Double Wasp R-2800-S1C4G engines with which the aircraft first flew in July 1941.

With this powerplant, a substantial production order was finally placed for the Warwick, the B Mk I with Wasp engines and the B Mk II with the Centaurus. However, the whole plan fell apart when the expected delivered of 400 Wasp engines from the US amounted to just 80. The Air Ministry contracts fell apart and only 16 production B Mk Is were ever built, none of them ever entered operational service.

Two B.1/95 prototypes, K8178 and L9704, and one B Mk II prototype, BV216, followed by 16 production aircraft serialled BV214, BV215, BV217–222, BV228–230, BV291, BV293, BV295 and BV296. The original order was placed on 28 December 1940 for 150 B Mk I and 100 B Mk IIs.

The second prototype went to serve Vickers as a development aircraft for several projects, including a trial for a pair of aft-firing barbettes, which would be fitted to the Windsor. The two barbettes, each fitted with a pair of machine guns, were controlled from the rear gunner's position. (Via Martyn Chorlton)

The first of two prototype Warwicks designed to B.1/35 and fitted with a pair of Rolls-Royce 24-cylinder X-type engines, which were later named Vultures. The under-developed engine was completely inadequate for the bomber, just as it had been for the Avro Manchester. (*Aeroplane*)

Warwick Prototypes, B Mk I & II	
ENGINE	(P1) Two Rolls-Royce Vulture I; (I) Two 1,850hp Pratt & Whitney Wasp R-2800-S1A4-G; (II) two 2,000hp Bristol Centaurus IV
WINGSPAN	96ft 8½in
LENGTH	70ft
HEIGHT	18ft 6in
WING AREA	1,019sq ft
GROSS WEIGHT	45,000lb
MAX SPEED	300mph at 20,000ft
SERVICE CEILING	28,200ft
RANGE	2,075 miles at 185mph at 15,000ft

Warwick C Mk I and C Mk III

Following the failure of the Warwick as a bomber, it was recognised from an early stage that the aircraft would be suited to the more passive role of troop transport and general duties. However, the idea lay dormant until 1942 when an order for 14 Warwicks was received from British Overseas Airways Corporation (BOAC).

The last of 14 Warwick C Mk Is delivered to BOAC in 1943 was ex-BV256, re-registered as G-AGFK. The aircraft was later transferred to 525 Squadron at Weston Zoyland, Somerset, and was not SOC until 29 July 1947. (Charles E Brown)

The plan was to have the entire order delivered to BOAC by the end of 1942 but this was to prove optimistic. A great deal of modification work was needed to convert the B Mk I into a C Mk I, including the removal of all military equipment and the installation of cabin windows, a strengthened freight floor, exhaust flame dampers and very long-range fuel tanks. The first aircraft, BV243, was first flown on 5 February 1943.

The development of the C Mk I, the C MK III, mainly differed in having a large ventral freight-pannier added in place of the bomb bay doors. These contained four 125-gallon fuel tanks.

The Warwick C Mk I first joined BOAC in 1943 and the type was employed to fly mail, freight and passengers from the British forces serving in North Africa at the time. Their service with the civilian airline was short and, by late 1944, all had been transferred to RAF Transport Command to serve with 167 Squadron base at Holmsley South, Hampshire.

The Warwick C Mk III first joined 46 and 47 Group, RAF Transport Command, which operated the type across the Mediterranean theatre, Italy and Greece from early 1945 to March 1946. The general serviceability rate of the Warwick was poor in RAF service, the aircraft seemingly unable to cope with the high temperatures, and this ruled it out of any Far-Eastern service.

The aircraft performed better in service between the United Kingdom and the Middle East and in this capacity the type joined 525 Squadron, operating out of Lyneham in June 1944 followed by 167 Squadron

Warwick C.III	
ENGINE	Two 1,850hp Pratt & Whitney Double Wasp R-2800-S1A4-G
WINGSPAN	96ft 8½in
LENGTH	70ft 6in
HEIGHT	18ft 6in
WING AREA	1,006sq ft
EMPTY WEIGHT	29,162lb
GROSS WEIGHT	46,000lb
MAX SPEED	260mph at 5,000ft
CLIMB RATE	675ft/min
SERVICE CEILING	15,000ft
RANGE	2,150 miles at 180mph at 15,000ft with 24 troops or 6,170lb load

at Blackbushe in November. The same month, the type was issued to 353 Squadron at Palem in India but the Warwick's fabric covering did not stand up well to the tropical conditions and the type was withdrawn in June 1945.

In the UK, two Polish units, 301 Squadron at Blackbushe, Hampshire, and 304 Squadron at North Weald, Essex, both of whom had been operating ex-BOAC C Mk Is, received the C Mk III in May and July 1945, respectively. 304 Squadron became the last unit to operate the Warwick – it replaced them with the Halifax C Mk VIII at Chedburgh, Suffolk, in May 1946.

Fourteen Warwick B Mk 1s were converted to C Mk 1 standard, initially serialled BV243–256 inclusive but re-registered as G-AGEX to G-AGFK in BOAC service. In total, 100 Warwick C Mk IIIs were built for the RAF serialled HG215–256, HG271–307 and HG320–340.

Warwick ASR Mk I and Mk VI

By early 1943, the Air Staff had made it clear that the Warwick did not have a future as a bomber but could be useful in the air-sea rescue (ASR) role and as a freighter. For the ASR role, the aircraft would have to be modified to carry Lindholme gear (five cylindrical containers, one with a nine-man dinghy and the rest with survival equipment) or an airborne lifeboat. By May 1943, an order for 100 Warwick ASRs had been placed.

The requirement of the Warwick ASR Mk I was simple; the aircraft must be able to carry two sets of Lindholme gear and/or a Mk I lifeboat and be able to drop it at a speed between 100 and 130mph. The aircraft must carry a crew of seven without oxygen equipment and when carrying the lifeboat, a specified range of 1,800 miles must be reached.

Achieving the numbers was no problem for the Warwick, and so a bespoke lifeboat needed to be created. Designed by Uffa Fox CBE, an English boat designer, the Mk I lifeboat was fitted with engines and rocket gear plus survival equipment but still only weighed in at 1,630lb. Before live testing, a 1/13 scale model was tested in an RAE wind tunnel, while a lifeboat was first dropped by a Hudson off Cowes with good results.

The first production version of the Warwick ASR was referred to as the Stage A, which was designed to carry, as originally specified, a lifeboat and two sets of Lindholme gear. Nine aircraft, beginning with BV298, were converted to this standard and trialled at Boscombe Down. Three Stage As were first to enter RAF service.

282 Squadron was reformed with Warwick ASR Mk I at Davidstow Moor on 1 February 1944. HF944, which remained with the unit until July 1946, is pictured around the time of the D-Day landings in June 1944. (Via Martyn Chorlton)

PN827, a Vickers Warwick Mk V, was retained by the manufacturer for ASR trials work until mid-1947. (Via Martyn Chorlton)

Warwick ASR Mk I	
ENGINE	Two 1,850hp Pratt & Whitney Double Wasp R-2800-S1A4-G
WINGSPAN	96ft 8½in
LENGTH	70ft 6in
HEIGHT	18ft 6in
WING AREA	1,006sq ft
EMPTY WEIGHT	28,154lb
GROSS WEIGHT	45,000lb
MAX SPEED	224mph at 3,600ft
CLIMB RATE	660ft/min
SERVICE CEILING	21,500ft
RANGE	2,300 miles at 150mph at 5,000ft

The Stage B, of which 20 were built, could also be fitted with ASV radar in the wing, had aerials mounted along the front fuselage and had an FN24 rear turret fitted. The finalised version of the Warwick ASR, the Stage C was redesignated as the ASR Mk I and encompassed both the A and B specifications. This mark could operate in four different layouts, firstly with a Mk I lifeboat at 42,924lb, Lindholme gear only at 41,534lb, a Mk II Lifeboat at 44,764lb and with extra fuel tanks with a potential range of 2,000 miles at 41,984lb.

The Warwick ASR Mk I entered service with 280 Squadron at Thornaby in October 1943 although three Stage As had already arrived in august while the unit was at Bircham Newton, Norfolk. The ASR Mk I went on to serve with 38, 251, 269, 276, 277–284, 292, 293 and 294 Squadrons, seven of these units were based in the UK and the remainder were stationed overseas.

The first successful Mk IA lifeboat drop by a Warwick took place on 9 January 1944 when it was dropped for a Mosquito crew off Land's End, Cornwall. On another occasion, a lifeboat was dropped to another Mosquito crew in the southern part of the Bay of Biscay; incredibly after four days at sea, the duo made it back home.

Nine Stage As were built, plus 20 Stage Bs, followed by 204 of the main production variant ASR Mk I with serials ranged from BV223 to HG214. In total, 94 of the mark, powered by Double Wasp R-2800-2SBG engines were built, although only two entered RAF service

Warwick GR Mk II, II Met and GR Mk V

The Warwick Mk II was given a new lease of life in the general reconnaissance role thanks to the increasing availability of the Bristol Centaurus engine. Two variants were planned as the main production types, one of which would be capable of carrying a pair of 18in or two 24in torpedoes and the other would be a radar-equipped variant complete with Leigh Light.

By May 1943, the Leigh Light version of what was to be designated the GR Mk II was cancelled. Instead, the aircraft, which was powered by a pair of Centaurus CE7SM engines, had provision for 12–15 depth charges and a dozen RPs in the early production aircraft. Another descendent of the Warwick Mk II was the GR (Met) Mk II, which was used for meteorological duties and high-altitude navigation training. All bomb gear was removed from Mets and the nose turret was removed and replaced by a wide-vision nose window; an oxygen system was also installed.

A product of the second batch of 109 GR Mk Vs built at Weybridge and delivered between May 1945 and April 1946, this aircraft, LM818, was one of a few that actually saw operational service, albeit in peacetime. The aircraft, complete with a clear Perspex ASV blister, (which appears to be empty) served with 179 Squadron, 1 FU and the TFU before it was retired in May 1950. (Via Martyn Chorlton)

The GR Mk V was the most successful of this group of Warwicks and was the first Centaurus-powered variant to enter service. The first aircraft, PN697, made its maiden flight in April 1944. The GR Mk V aircraft was similar to the GR Mk II but was fitted with a radar scanner under the nose and a Leigh Light, installed at a fixed inclination of seven degrees, in the ventral position. The mid-upper turret was also removed and a pair of 0.5in Browning machine guns was fitted into the beam position instead. Initially, directional instability problems were cured by fitting a dorsal fin in front of the main fin.

Warwick B.II	
ENGINE	Two 2,500hp Bristol Centaurus VI
WINGSPAN	96ft 8½in
LENGTH	68ft 6in
HEIGHT	18ft 6in
WING AREA	1,006sq ft
EMPTY WEIGHT	31,125lb
GROSS WEIGHT	51,250lb
MAX SPEED	262mph at 2,000ft
SERVICE CEILING	19,000ft
RANGE	3,050 miles at 161mph at 5,000ft

269 Squadron groundcrew load a Warwick ASR.1 (Stage A) with a Mk 1 Lifeboat at Lagens, Azores, in 1945. A straight conversion from the Warwick B Mk 1, the Stage A aircraft were dedicated ASR machines, not only carrying the lifeboat but also two sets of Lindholme gear. (IWM via Martyn Chorlton)

The second production Vickers Warwick GR Mk V, PN698, during trials with the A&AEE, out of Boscombe Down in 1944. The aircraft never joined an operational unit and was SOC on 20 August 1947. (via Martyn Chorlton)

The GR Mk II never entered operational service but was allocated to 6 and 26 OTU and the Empire Air Navigational School, although the odd aircraft did briefly serve with 38 and 524 Squadrons. The few GR (Met) Mk IIs built did not enter operational service but the GR Mk V did, first joining 179 Squadron at St Eval, North Cornwall, in November 1944. 621 Squadron also operated the GR Mk V from Mersa Matruh, Egypt, from January 1945 and, had the war lasted longer, the aircraft would have been delivered to many more units.

Post-war, 32 GR Mk Vs also served with 17 and 27 Squadrons, South African Air Force (SAAF) from May 1945 to March 1946 and March to December 1945 respectively. The aircraft of 179 Squadron were retired in May 1946 and 621 Squadron in August 1946. Both RAF units were re-equipped with Lancaster GR Mk III.

Aircraft produced included 119 GR Mk IIs (HG341–512), 14 GR (Met) Mk IIs (HG513–525 and HG533–539) and 236 GR Mk Vs (ranging from LM777 to PN682); a follow-on order for 116 GR Mk VIs was cancelled.

Chapter 14

Wimpy Units

Royal Air Force

First-line

8 Sqn	*Uspiam et passim (Everywhere unbounded)*	
A/c	Mk XIII	Dec 1943 to May 1945
Code	'A'	
Base	Khormaksar	

9 Sqn	*Per noctum volamus (We fly by night)*	
A/c:	Mk I	Jan to Dec 1939
	Mk IA	Sep 1939 to Sep 1940
Mk IC		Feb 1940 to Oct 1941
Mk II		Mar 1941 to Aug 1942
Mk III		Jul 1941 to Jun1942
Code:	WS	Sep 1939 to Apr 1951
Bases:	Honington and Lossiemouth	

12 Sqn	*Leads the Field*	
A/c:	Mk II	Nov 1940 to Nov 1942
	Mk III	Aug to Nov 1942
Code:	PH	Sep 1939 to Apr 1951
Bases:	Binbrook, Thruxton and Wickenby	

14 Sqn	*I spread my wings and keep my promise*	
A/c:	Mk XIV	Nov 1944 to May 945
Code:	CX	Sep 1944 to Jun 1945
Base:	Chivenor	

A trio of 37 Squadron Wellington Mk ICs somewhere over North Africa in early 1941. Originally equipped with the Harrow when it reformed at Feltwell in April 1937, the unit went on to operate the Wellington from May 1939 through to October 1944 when the Liberator took over. (*Aeroplane*)

15 Sqn *Aim Sure*
A/c: Mk IC   Nov 1940 to May 1941
Code: LS   Sep 1939 to Apr 1951
Base: Wyton

24 (Commonwealth) Sqn   *In Omnia Paratus (Ready in all things)*
A/c: Mk XVI   Feb 1943 to Jan 1944
Codes: ZK   Apr 1941 to 1943
     NQ   1943 to 1946
Base: Northolt

36 Sqn *Rajawali raja langit (Eagle King of the sky)*
A/c: Mk IC   Dec 1942 to Jul 1943
     Mk VIII   Feb to Sep 1943
     Mk X   Jun to Nov 1943
     Mk XI   Jul to Sep 1943
     Mk XII   Jul to Dec 1943
     Mk XIII   Jul to Dec 1943
     Mk XIV   Sep 1943 to Jun 1945
Code: RW   Oct 1944 to Jun 1945
Bases: Tanjore, Dhubalia, Blida, Bone, Montecorvino, La Senia, Gibraltar, Tafaraoui, Grottaglie, Bo Rizzo, Ghisonaccia, Reghaia, Alghero, Tarquinia, Chivenor and Benbecula

37 Sqn *Wise without eyes*
A/c: Mk I   May 1939 to Nov 1939
     Mk IA   Oct 1939 to Aug 40
     Mk IC   Jun 1940 to Apr 1943
     Mk III   Mar to Apr 1943
     Mk X   Mar 1943 to Oct 1944

9 Squadron shows off its new Wellington Mk Is in early 1939.

Codes: FJ   Apr to Sep 1939

	Code	Period
Codes:	FJ	Apr to Sep 1939
	LF	Sep 1939 to Mar 1946

Bases: Feltwell, Salon, Luqa, Fayid, Shallufa, Menidi, Paramythia, Shaibah, LG 76, LG 09, Luqa, LG 224, Abu Sueir, LG 106, LG 140, Benina, El Magrun, Gardabia East, Gardabia West, Kairouan, Djedeida, Cerignola and Tortorella

38 Sqn   *Ante lucem (Before the dawn)*

A/c:	Aircraft	Period
A/c:	Mk I	Nov 1938 to Apr1940
	Mk IA	Sep 1939 to Jun 1940
	Mk IC	Apr 1940 to Aug 1942
	Mk II	Aug to Oct 1941
	Mk VIII	May 1942 to Sep 1943
	Mk XI	Jun 1943 to May 1944
	Mk XII	Jun to Sep 1943
	Mk XIII	Sep 1943 to Jan 1945
	Mk XIV	Jan 1945 to Dec 1946
Codes:	NH	Dec 1938 to Sep 1939
	HD	Sep 1939 to 1942
	RL	Jun 1946 to 1949

Bases: Marham, Ismailia, Fayid, LG 60, Shallufa, Gambut, Sidi Azeiz, Fuka, Elevsis, El Adem, Luqa, LG 117, LG 09, LG 226, Berka III, Gianaclis, Misurata, LG 91, St Jean, Kalamaki, Grottaglie, Foggia Main, Rosignano, Hal Far and Falconara

40 Sqn   *Hostem coelo expellere (To drive the enemy from the sky)*

A/c:	Aircraft	Period
A/c:	Mk IC	Nov 1940 to Feb 1942
		May 1942 to Jun 1943
	Mk III	Mar 1943 to Apr 1944
	Mk X	May 1943 to Mar 1945
Code:	BL	Sep 1939 to Apr 1947

Bases: Wyton, Abu Sueir, Shallufa, Kabrit, LG 222A, LG 104, Luqa, LG 237, Heliopolis, El Magrun, Gardabia East, Gardabia West, El Alem East, Hani West, Oudna No.1, Cerignola No.2 and Foggia Main

57 Sqn   *Corpus non animum muto (I change my body not my spirit)*

A/c:	Aircraft	Period
A/c:	Mk IA	Nov 1940
	Mk IC	Nov 1940 to Jun 1942
	Mk II	Jul to Nov 1941
	Mk III	Jan to Sep 1942
Code:	DX	Apr 1940 to Apr 1951
Base:	Feltwell	

69 Sqn   *With vigilance we serve*

A/c:	Aircraft	Period
A/c:	Mk VIII	Aug 1942 to Feb 1943
	Mk XIII	May 1944 to Aug 1945
Code:	–	

Bases: Luqa, Montecorvino, Northolt, A12/Balleroy, B48/Amiens/Glisy, B58 Melsbroek, B78/Endhoven and Aalborg

70 Sqn   *Usquam (Anywhere)*

A/c: Mk IC   Sep 1940 to Jan 1943

        Mk III   Jan to Nov 1943

        Mk X   Apr 1943 to Jan 1945

Code: –

Base: Kabrit, Tatoi, El Adem, Shaibah, LG 75, LG 104, LG 224, Abu Sueir, LG 106, LG 140, Benina, El Magrun, Gardabia East, Gardabia West, Temmar, Djedeida, Cerignola and Tortorella

75 (New Zealand) Sqn *Ake Ake Kia Kaha (For ever and ever be strong)*

A/c: Mk I   Apr to Aug 1940

        Mk IA   Apr to Aug 1940

        Mk IC   May 1940 to Jan 1942

        Mk III   Jan to Nov 1942

Code: AA   Apr 1940 to Oct 1945

Bases: Feltwell, Salon, Mildenhall, Oakington and Newmarket

93 Sqn   *Ad arma parati (Ready for battle)*

A/c: Mk IC   Mar to Jul 1941

Code: HN   Dec 1940 to Nov 1941

Base: Middle Wallop

99 (Madras Presidency) Sqn   *Quisque tenax (Each one tenacious)*

A/c: Mk I   Oct 1938 to Dec 1939

        Mk IA   Sep 1939 to Apr 1940

        Mk IC   Mar 1940 to Feb 1942

                        Oct to May 1943

        Mk II   Jul to Oct 1941

        Mk III   Apr 1943 to Aug 1944

        Mk X   Apr 1943 to Aug 1944

Code: VF   Apr to Sep 1939

        LN   Sep 1939 to Feb 1942

Bases: Mildenhall, Newmarket, Lossiemouth, Salon, Waterbeach, Ambala, Solan, Pandeveswar, Digri, Chaklala, Jessore, Agartala, and Kumbhirgram

101 Sqn   *Mens agitat molem (Mind over matter)*

A/c: Mk IC   Apr 1941 to Feb 1942

        Mk III   Feb to Oct 1942

Code: SR   Sept 1939 to Apr 1951

Bases: West Raynham, Oakington, Bourn, Stradishall and Holme-on-Spalding Moor

103 Sqn   *Noli me tangere (Touch me not)*

A/c: Mk IC   Oct 1940 to Jul 1942

Code: PM   Sep 1939 to Nov 1945

Bases: Newton and Elsham Wolds

104 Sqn   *Strike hard*
A/c: Mk II   Apr 1941 to Aug 1943
          Mk X   Jul 1943 to Feb 1945
Code   EP   Sep 1939 to Apr 1947
Bases   Driffield, Kabrit, LG 106, Luqa, LG 224, LG 104, LG 237, Soluch, Gardabia Main, Cheria, Hani West, Oudna, Cerignola No.3, and Foggia Main

108 Sqn   *Viribus contractis (With gathering strength)*
A/c: Mk IC   Aug 1941 to Nov 1942
Code: –
Bases: Kabrit, Fayid, LG 09 and LG 105

109 Sqn   *Primi hastate (The first of the legion)*
A/c: Mk IC   Dec 1940 to Dec 1942
          Mk I   Jul to Sep 1941
          Mk VI   Mar to Jul 1942
Code: HS   Dec 1940 to Apr 1945
Bases: Boscombe Down, Tempsford, Wyton, Upper Heyford and Stradishall

115 Sqn   *Despite the elements*
A/c: Mk I   Mar to Oct 1939
          Mk IA   Sep 1939 to Aug 1940
          Mk IC   Jun 1940 to Feb 1942
          Mk III   Feb 1942 to Mar 1943

38 Squadron Wellington GR Mk VIII four-ship off the Italian coast, possibly while operating out of Foggia Main.

Code:	BK	Apr to Sep 1939
	KO	Sep 1939 to Mar 1950
Bases:	Marham, Kinloss, Mildenhall and East Wretham	

142 Sqn *Determination*

A/c:	Mk II	Nov 1940 to Oct 1941
	Mk IV	Oct 1941 to Sep 1942
	Mk III	Sep 1942 to Aug 1943
	Mk X	Jun 1943 to Oct 1944
Code:	QT	Sep 1939 to Oct 1944
Bases:	Binbrook, Waltham, Blida, Kirmington, Fontaine Chaude, Kairouan, Oudna, Cerigola No.3, Amendola and Regina	

148 Sqn *Trusty*

A/c:	Mk IC	Apr to May 1940
		Dec 1940 to Oct 1941
		Apr to Dec 1942
	Mk II	Oct 1941 to Apr 1942
Code:	–	
Bases:	Stradishall, Luqa, Kabrit, LG 60, LG 104, LG 106, LG 237, LG 09, LG 167 and Kilo 40	

149 (East India) Sqn *Fortis nocte (Strong by night)*

A/c:	Mk I	Jan to Dec 1939
	Mk IA	Sep 1939 to Jun 1940
	Mk IC	Mar 1939 to Dec 1941
Code:	LY	Jan to Sep 1939
	OJ	Sep 1939 to Mar 1950
Bases:	Mildenhall and Salon	

150 Sqn *AIEI ΦΘANOMEN (Always ahead)*

A/c:	Mk IA	Oct to Dec 1940
	Mk IC	Oct 1940 to Dec 1942
	Mk III	Sep 1942 to Aug 1943
	Mk X	Apr 1943 to Oct 1944
Code:	JN	Sep 1939 to Oct 1944
Bases:	Newton, Snaith, Kirmington, Blida, Fontaine Chaude, Kairouan West, Oudna No.2, Cerignola No.3, Amendola and Regina	

156 Sqn *We light the way*

A/c:	Mk IC	Feb to Jun 1942
	Mk III	Feb 1942 to Jan 1943
Code:	GT	Feb 1942 to Sep 1945
Bases:	Alconbury and Warboys	

158 Sqn *Strength in unity*

A/c:	Mk II	Feb to Jun 1942

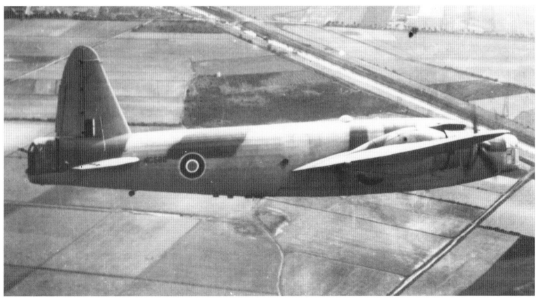

Wellington GR Mk XIII, NC588, of 69 Squadron, a unit that operated this mark between May 1944 and August 1945, although this particular aircraft was not SOC until May 1947.

Code:	NP	Apr 1942 to Jun 1945
Base:	Driffield	

162 Sqn *One time, one purpose*

A/c:	Mk IC	Jan 1942 to Feb 1944
	Mk III	Sep to Nov 1943
		Jan to Jul 1944
	Mk DW I	Mar to Jul 1944
	Mk X	Apr to Sep 1944
Code:	–	
Bases:	LG 91, Idku, Lakatamia, St Jean and Benina	

166 Sqn *Tenacity*

A/c:	Mk III	Jan to Apr 1943
	Mk X	Feb to Sep 1943
Code:	AS	Jan 1943 to Nov 1945
Base:	Kirmington	

172 Sqn *Insidiantibus insidiamur (We ambush the ambushers)*

A/c:	Mk VIII	Apr 1942 to Mar 1943
	Mk XII	Dec 1942 to Oct 1943
	Mk XIV	Aug 1943 to Jun 1945
Code:	WN	1942 to 1943
	I	Aug 1943 to Jul 1944
	OG	Jul 1944 to Jun 1945
Bases:	Chivenor, Skitten, Lagens, Gibraltar and Limavady	

70 Squadron Wellington Mk X, HE627, which failed to return from a raid on Ferentino, Italy, on 23 May 1944.

179 Sqn *Delentem deleo (I destroy the destroyer)*
A/c: Mk VIII   Sep 1942 to Sep 1943
            Mk XIV   Aug 1943 to Nov 1944
Code: –
Bases: Skitten, Gibraltar, Agadir, Blida, Lagens, Predannack, Chivenor, Benbecula and St Eval

192 Sqn *Dare to discover*
A/c: Mk IC   Jan to Mar 1943
            Mk III   Jan to Mar 1943
            Mk X   Jan 1943 to Jan 1945
Code: DT   Jan 1943 to Aug 1945
Bases: Gransden Lodge, Feltwell and Foulsham

196 Sqn *Sic fidem servamus (Thus we keep the faith)*
A/c: Mk III   Dec 1942
            Mk X   Dec 1942 to Jul 1943
Code: ZO   Nov 1942 to Mar 1946
Base: Leconfield

199 Sqn *Let tyrants tremble*
A/c: Mk III   Nov 1942 to Apr 1943
            Mk X   Mar to Jun 1943
Code: EX   Nov 1942 to Jul 1945
Bases: Blyton and Ingham

203 Sqn *Occidens oriensque (West and East)*
A/c: Mk XIII   Nov 1943 to Oct 1944
Code: –
Base: Santa Cruz

214 (Federated Malay States) Sqn
Ulter in umbris (Avenging in the shadows)

A/c:	Mk I	May 1939 to May 1940
	Mk IA	Sep 1939 to Sep 1940
	Mk IC	Jul 1940 to Apr 1942
	Mk II	Nov to Dec 1941
Code:	UX	Apr to Sep 1939
	BU	Sep 1939 to Jul 1945
Bases:	Feltwell, Methwold, Stradishall and Honington	

215 Sqn
Surgite nox adest (Arise, night is at hand)

A/c:	Mk I	Jul 1939 to Apr 1940
	Mk IA	Apr to May 1940
	Mk IC	Feb 1942 to Sep 1943
	Mk X	Sep 1943 to Aug 1944
Code:	–	
Bases:	Honington, Bramcote, Bassingbourn, Silloth, Jurby, Squires Gate, Harwell, Newmarket, Waterbeach, Asansol, Pandeveswar, Dum Dum, Alipore, St Thomas Mount, Vizagapatam, Chaklala, Jessore, Digri, Chittagong, Cuttack, Kolar and Armada Road	

218 (Gold Coast) Sqn
In Time

A/c:	Mk IC	Nov 1940 to Feb 1942
	Mk II	May to Dec 1941
Code:	HA	Sep 1939 to Aug 1945
Bases:	Oakington and Marham	

X3595 joined 75 (NZ) Squadron as a Mk III but is pictured after conversion to a Mk X in May 1942. 75 Squadron never operated the Mk X but the unit's codes still remain.

221 Sqn *From sea to sea*

A/c:	Mk IC	Nov 1940 to Dec 1941
	Mk VIII	Jan 1942 to Sep 1943
	Mk XI	Jun to Dec 1943
	Mk XII	Sep to Oct 1943
	Mk XIII	Oct 1943 to Aug 1945
Code:	DF	Nov 1940 to Jan 1942

Bases: Bircham Newton, Limavady, St Eval, Reykjavik, Docking, LG 39, Luqa, LG 87, LG 05, LG 99, Shandur, Gianaclis, St Jean, Shallufa, Idku, LG 143, Berka II, Grottaglie, Foggia, Kalamaki/ Hassani, Idku, Aqir, El Adem and Benina

232 Sqn *Strike*

A/c:	Mk XVI	Dec 1944 to Feb 1945
Code:	–	
Base:	Stoney Cross	

242 (Canadian) Sqn *Toujour Prêt (Always ready)*

A/c:	Mk XVI	Jan to Feb 1945
Code:	–	
Base:	Stoney Cross	

244 Sqn

A/c:	Mk XIII	Feb 1944 to May 1945
Code:	–	
Base:	Sharjah, Masirah, Khormaksar, Mogadishu and Santa Cruz	

281 Sqn *Volamus servaturi (We fly to save)*

A/c:	Mk XIII	Aug to Sep 1945
Code:	FA	Mar 1942 to Oct 1945
Bases:	Ballykelly, Tiree and Tain	

294 Sqn *Vita ex undis abrepta (Life snatched from the waves)*

A/c:	Mk IC	Sep 1943 to Mar 1944
	Mk XI	Mar 1944 to Jun 1945
	Mk XIII	Jun 1944 to Apr 1946
Code:	–	

Bases: Berka, LG 07, Lakatamia, MellahaLimassol, Derna, Gambut, LG 91, Berka III, St Jean, Castel Benito, Idku, Gambut No.3, Ramat David, Luxor, Benina, El Adem, Aboukir, Nicosia, Aqir, Hassani, Lydda, Basrah, Sharjah, Masirah and Muharraq

300 (Masovian) Sqn

A/c:	Mk IC	Dec 1940 to Sep 1941
	Mk IV	Aug 1941 to Jan 1943
	Mk III	Jan to Apr 1943
	Mk X	Mar 1943 to Mar 1944
Code:	BH	Jul 1940 to Oct 1946

149 Squadron Wellington Mk Is over Paris on Bastille Day on 14 July 1939. (Charles E Brown via *Aeroplane*)

Bases: Bramcote, Swinderby, Hemswell, Ingham and Faldingworth

301 (Pomeranian) Sqn

A/c:	Mk IC	Oct 1940 to Aug 1941
	Mk IV	Aug 1941 to Apr 1943
Code:	GR	Jul 1940 to Apr 1943
Bases:	Swinderby and Hemswell	

304 (Silesian) Sqn

A/c:	Mk IC	Nov 1940 to Apr 1943
	Mk X	Apr to Jun 1943
	Mk XIII	Jun to Sep 1943
	Mk XIV	Sep 1943 to Dec 1945
Codes:	NZ	Aug 1940 to May 1942
	'2'	Aug 1943 to Jul 1944
	QD	Jul 1944 to Dec 1946

Bases: Bramcote, Syerston, Lindholme, Tiree, Dale, Talbenny, Dale, Docking, Davidstow Moor, Predannock, Chivenor, Benbecula, Limavady, St Eval, North Weald and Chedburgh

305 (Wielpolska) Sqn

A/c:	Mk IC	Nov 1940 to Jul 1941
	Mk II	Jul 1941 to Aug 1942
	Mk IV	Aug 1942 to May 1943
	Mk X	May to Aug 1943
Code:	SM	Aug 1940 to Jan 1947
Bases:	Bramcote, Syerston, Lindholme, Hemswell and Ingham	

311 (Czechoslovak) Sqn   *Na mnozstvi nehledte (Never regard their numbers)*

A/c:	Mk IC	Aug 1940 to Jun 1943
Code:	KX	Jul 1940 to Apr 1942
Bases:	Honington, East Wretham, Stradishall, Aldergrove, Talbenny and Beaulieu	

344 (Flotille 1E) Free French Sqn

A/c:	Mk XI	Nov 1943 to Nov 1945
	Mk XIII	Nov 1943 to Nov 1945
Code:	–	
Bases:	Dakar and Port Etienne	

405 (Vancouver) Sqn, RCAF   *Ducimus (We lead)*

A/c:	Mk II	May 1941 to Apr 1942
Code:	LQ	Apr 1941 to Sep 1945
Bases:	Driffield and Pocklington	

407 (Demon) Sqn, RCAF   *To hold on high*

A/c:	Mk XI	Jan to Apr 1943
	Mk XII	Mar to Feb 1944

Codes:	Mk XIV	Jun 1943 to Jun 1945
	RR	May 1941 to Aug 1943
	'1'	Aug 1943 to Jan 1944
	'2'	Jan to Jul 1944
	'C1'	Jul 1944 to 1945
Bases:	Docking, Skitten, Chivenor, St Eval, Limavady and Wick	

415 (Swordfish) Sqn, RCAF   *Ad metam (To the mark)*

A/c:	Mk XIII	Sep 1943 to Jul 1944
Code:	GX	Aug 1941 to Oct 1943
	NH	Oct 1943 to Jul 1944
Bases:	Thorney Island, Bircham Newton, North Coates, Docking and East Moor	

419 (Moose) Sqn, RCAF   *Moosa aswayita (Beware the moose)*

A/c:	Mk IC	Jan to Nov 1942
	Mk III	Feb to Nov 1942
Code:	–	
Bases:	Mildenhall, Leeming, Topcliffe, Croft and Middleton St George	

420 (Snowy Owl) Sqn, RCAF   *Pugnamus finitum (We fight to the finish)*

A/c:	Mk III	Aug 1942 to Apr 1943
	Mk X	Feb to Oct 1943
Code:	PT	Dec 1941 to Sep 1945
Bases:	Skipton-on-Swale, Middleton St George, Kairouan and Hani East	

301 (Pomeranian) Squadron Wellington Mk IC, R1006, being bombed up at Swinderby in early 1941. The aircraft later served 21 and 18 OTUs, succumbing to an engine fire on approach to Bramcote with the latter.

424 (Tiger) Sqn, RCAF   *Castigandos castigamus (We chastise those who deserve to be chastised)*

A/c:	Mk III	Oct 1942 to Apr 1943
	Mk X	Feb to Oct 1943
Code:	QB	Oct 1942 to Oct 1945
Bases:	Topcliffe, Leeming, Dalton, Kairouan and Hani East	

425 (Alouette) Sqn, RCAF   *Je te plumerai (I shall pluck you)*

A/c:	Mk III	Aug 1942 to Apr 1943
	Mk X	Apr to Oct 1943
Code:	KW	Jun 1942 to Sep 1945
Bases:	Dishforth, Kairouan and Hani East	

426 (Thunderbird) Sqn, RCAF   *On wings of fire*

A/c:	Mk III	Oct 1942 to Apr 1943
	Mk X	Mar to Jun 1943
Code:	OW	Oct 1942 to Dec 1945
Bases:	Dishforth and Linton-on-Ouse	

427 (Lion) Sqn, RCAF   *Ferte manus certas (Strike sure)*

A/c:	Mk III	Nov 1942 to Mar 1943
	Mk X	Feb 1943 to May 1943
Code:	ZL	Nov 1942 to May 1946
Base:	Croft	

428 (Ghost) Sqn, RCAF   *Usque ad finem (To the very end)*

A/c:	Mk III	Nov 1942 to Apr 1943
	Mk X	Apr to Jun 1943
Code:	NA	Nov 1942 to May 1946
Base:	Dalton	

429 (Bison) Sqn, RCAF   *Fortunae nihil (Nothing to chance)*

A/c:	Mk III	Nov 1942 to Aug 1943
	Mk X	Jan to Aug19 43
Code:	–	
Base:	East Moor	

431 (Iroquois) Sqn, RCAF   *The hatitan ronterios (Warriors of the air)*

A/c:	Mk X	Dec 1942 to Jul 1943
Code:	SE	Nov 1942 to Sep 1945
Base:	Burn	

432 (Leaside) Sqn, RCAF   *Saeviter ad lucem (Ferociously towards the light)*

A/c:	Mk X	May to Nov 1943
Code:	QO	May 1943 to May 1945
Bases:	Skipton-on-Swale and East Moor	

Affectionately known as the 'Wimpy' in RAF circles, the Vickers Wellington was also known as the 'basketweave' bomber because of the complex geodetic system, designed by Barnes, which was used for virtually its entire construction. This image is taken above the bomb bay looking towards the rear fuselage and turret position at Weybridge in December 1939. (*Aeroplane*)

458 Sqn, RAAF

A/c:	Mk IV	Aug 1941 to Jan 1942
	Mk IC	Feb to Apr 1942
		Sep to Nov 1942
	Mk VIII	Sep 1942 to Sep 1943
	Mk XIII	Jun 1943 to May 1944
	Mk XIV	Jan 1944 to Jun 1945
Code:	MD	Oct 1942 to Apr 1943

Bases: Holme-on-Spalding Moor, Kabrit, Abu Sueir, Shallufa, Gambut, Berka, Luqa, LG 91, Blida, Protville, Bone, Grottaglie, Ghisonaccia, Bo Rizzo, Reghaia, Alghero, Foggia, Falconara, Le Vallon, Rosignano and Gibraltar

460 Sqn, RAAF   *Strike and return*

A/c:	Mk IV	Nov 1941 to Sep 1942
Code:	UV	Nov 1941 to May 1943

Bases: Molesworth and Breighton

466 Sqn, RAAF

A/c:	Mk II	Oct to Nov 1942
	Mk X	Nov 1942 to Sep 1943
Code:	HD	Oct 1942 to Oct 1945

Bases: Driffield and Leconfield

524 Sqn

A/c:	Mk XIII	Apr 1944 to Jan 1945
	Mk XIV	Dec 1944 to May 1945
Code:	'7R'	Apr 1944 to May 1945

Bases: Davidstow Moor, Docking, Bircham Newton and Langham

527 Sqn   *Silently we serve*

A/c:	Mk X	Apr 1945 to Apr 1946
Code:	WN	Jun 1943 to Apr 1946

Bases: Digby and Watton

544 Sqn   *Quero (I seek)*

A/c:	Mk IV	Oct 1942 to Mar 1943
Code:	–	

Base: Benson

547 Sqn   *Celer ad caedendum (Swift to strike)*

A/c:	Mk VIII	Oct 1942 to May 1943
	Mk XI	May to Nov 1943
	Mk XIII	Oct to Nov 1943
Code:	2V	Aug 1943 to Jun 1945

Bases: Holmsley South, Chivenor, Tain, Davidstow Moor and Thorney Island

612 (County of Aberdeen) Sqn   *Vigilando custodimus (We stand guard by vigilance)*

A/c:	Mk VIII	Nov 1942 to Mar 1943
	Mk XIII	Mar 1943 to Mar 1944
	Mk XIV	Jun 1943 to Jul 1945
Code:	WL	Sep 1939 to Aug 1943
	8W	Jul 1944 to Jul 1945
Bases:	Wick, Davidstow Moor, Chivenor, St Eval, Limavady and Langham	

621 Sqn   *Every Ready to Strike*

A/c:	Mk XIII	Sep 1943 to Nov 1945
	Mk XIV	Jan to Dec 1945
Code:	–	
Bases:	Port Reitz, Mogadishu, Scuscuiban, Bandar Kassim, Riyan, Khormaksar, Socotra and Mersah Matruh	

Fleet Air Arm

716 Sqn

A/c:	Mk XI	Jul 1944 to Aug 1945
Code:	–	
Base:	Eastleigh	

728 Sqn

A/c:	Mk XIV	1946
Code:	HF	
Base:	Ta Kali, Luqa and Hal Far	

758 Sqn

A/c:	Mk XI	Sep to Dec 1943
Code:	U3	
Base:	Hinstock	

762 Sqn

A/c:	Mk XI	Aug 1944 to Apr 1945
Code:	–	
Base:	Dale	

765 Sqn

A/c:	Mk X	Jul 1945 to Apr 1946
	Mk XI	Aug 1944 to Apr 1946
Code:		
Base:	Lee-on-Solent, Hornchurch, Manston and Hal Far	

783 Sqn

A/c:	Mk I	Feb to Sep 1944
	Mk II	Feb to Sep 1944
Code:	AO	
Base:	Arbroath	

RAF SECOND-LINE UNITS

Aden Communication Flt; Advanced B&GS (Middle East); 201 AFS; 202 AFS; 15 (P)AFU; 20 (P)AFU; Mk X AI Conversion Flt; 1 AAS; AFEE; Airborne Forces Tactical Development Unit; Airborne Transport Tactical Development Unit; Aircraft Torpedo Development Unit; Aircrew Transit Pool; Air Fighting Development Establishment; Air Fighting Training Unit; 1 AGS; 2 AGS; 3 AGS; 10 AGS; 11 AGS; 12 AGS; Air Gunnery & Bombing School; Air Landing School (India); Air Navigation School; Air Navigation & Bombing School; 1 ANS; 2 ANS; 5 ANS; 6 ANS; 7 ANS; 10 ANS; Air Photographic Development Unit; 1 (North Africa) ASR Flt; ASR & Communication Flt; Air-Sea Warfare Development Unit; Air-Sea Warfare Development Unit (ACSEA); ASV Training Flt/Unit; Air Transport Auxiliary Advanced FTS; 26 AACU; 21 APC; Armament Synthetic Development Unit; RAF Austria Commission Communication Flt; RAF Bengal/Burma Communication Sqn; The Bomber Command Instructor's School; Bomber Development Unit; Bombing Development Unit; British Airways Repair Unit (Middle East); Central Fighter Establishment; Central Gunnery School; Central Navigation School; Central Navigation & Control School; Central Signals Establishment; Coastal Command Development Unit; Coastal Command Flying Instructors School; Coastal Command Preparation School; 1 (Coastal) Engine Control Demonstration Unit; 1331 CU; 1380 CU; 1381 (Transport) CU; 1692 (Bomber Support) Training Unit; Czechoslovak Flt; Empire Air Armament School; Empire Air Navigation School; Empire Central Flying School; Empire Flying School; (No.1) Engine Consumption Unit; No.1 Engine Control and Demonstration Unit; Engine Control Instructional Flight; No.2 (Middle East) Ferry Control; 21 Ferry Control; 22 Ferry Control; 1 Ferry Crew Pool; 3 Ferry Pool; Ferry Training and Despatch Flight; Ferry Training Unit; 301 Ferry Training Unit; 303 FTU; 304 FTU; 307 FTU; 310 FTU; 311 FTU; 312 FTU; 1 Ferry Unit; 3 FU; 8 FU; 11 FU; 12 FU; Fighter Experimental Establishment; Fighter Interception Development Unit; Fighter Interception Unit; 3 Film Reproduction Unit; 1302 Meteorological Flight; 417 (General Reconnaissance) Flt; 420 Flt; 1418 Flt; 1422 (Night Fighter) Flt; 1425 Flt; 1429 (Czech Operational Training) Flt; 1443 Flt; 1446 Flt; 1473 Flt; 1474 Flt; 1481 (Target Towing) Flt; 1482 (Target Towing) Flt; 1483 (Target Towing) Flt; 1485 (Target Towing) Flt; 4 Beam Approach Training Flight (BATF); 5 BATF; 8 BATF; 9 BATF; 10 BATF; 1503 BATF; 1504 BATF; 1505 BATF; 1508 BATF; 1509 BATF; 1510 BATF; 1572 Ground Gunnery Flt; 1577 Flt; 1680 (Western Isles) Flt; 1688 (Bomber) Defence Training Flt; 1689 (Ferry Training) Flt; 1690 (Bomber) Defence Training Flt; 1692 (Radar Development) Flt; 7 Flying Instructors School; 11 FIS; 12 (Operational) FIS; Flying Refresher School; 101 FRS; 104 FRS; 2 (Bomber) Forward Repair Depot; RAF Training Delegation (France); 2 French Technical Liaison Unit; Groupe 'Artois'; General Reconnaissance Aircraft Preparation School; 2 School of General Reconnaissance; 1 General Reconnaissance Unit; 2 GRU; 3 GRU; Glider Test and Ferry Unit (5 MU); Glider Test and Ferry Unit (6 MU); Air Headquarters Greece Flt; 38 Group Communication Flt; 60 Gp CF; 87 Gp CF; 92 Gp CF; 201 Gp CF; 205 Gp CF; 216 Gp CF; 218 Gp CF; 224 Gp CF; 2 Group Disbandment Centre; 92 Group Instructors Course/School/Flt; 93 Group Servicing Section/Flt; 5 Gp TTF; 3 Group Training Flt; 5 Gp TF; 205 Gp TF; Gunnery Research Unit; 1 Heavy Glider Servicing Unit; High Altitude Flt (A&AEE); Communication Flt Iraq and Persia; Air Headquarters Italy Communication Sqn/Flt; Communication Flt, Khartoum; Air Headquarters Levant Communication Flt; LORAN Training Unit; Communication Flt, Lydda; 30 Maintenance Unit; 46 MU; Air Headquarters Malta CF; Malta Communications and Target Towing Sqn; Malta Wellington Flt; Mediterranean Allied

Coastal Air Forces CF; Mediterranean and Middle East Communications Sqn; Metropolitan Communication Sqn; Air Headquarters Middle East Communications Flt/Unit; Middle East Communication Sqn; 2 Middle East Training School; 3 Middle East Training Unit;4 Middle East Training Unit; 5 Middle East Training Unit; New Zealand Flt; Night Fighter Leaders School; 2 Officers Advanced Training School; 228 Operational Conversion Unit; 237 OCU; 1 (Coastal) Operational Training Unit; 3 (C)OTU; 5, 6, 7, 10, 11, 12, 14, 15, 16, 17, 18, 19, 20, 21, 22, 23, 24, 25, 26, 27, 28, 29, 30, 51, 62, 63, 75, 76, 77, 78, 81, 82, 83, 84, 85, 86 and 104 (Glider) OTU; 105 (Glider) OTU; 111 (Coastal) OTU; Overseas Aircraft Despatch Unit (OADU); 1 OADU; 3 OADU; Overseas Aircraft Preparation Flt/Unit (OAPU); 1 Overseas Aircraft Preparation Unit; 3 OAPU; 4 OAPU; (No.1) Parachute Training School; 4 Parachute Training School; Photographic Reconnaissance Development Unit; Photographic Reconnaissance Unit; 3 PRU; 1 (Pilot) Refresher Flying Unit; Pilot Training Unit & Reinforcement Pool; Polish Flt; Power Jets Unit; Radar Training Flt (later 1 Radar Training Flt); 1 Radio Fitting Unit; Radio Warfare Establishment; 3 RFU; 4 RFU; 57 Repair & Salvage Unit; 108 Repair & Salvage Unit; 428 Repair & Salvage Unit; Research Department Flt; 1 Reserve Aircraft Pool (Bombers); RAE; RAF Flying College; Sea Rescue Flt; 16 Servicing Flt; 3502 Serving Unit; 3054 SU; 3507 (AAC) SU; Signals Development Unit; Signals Flying Unit; Signals Sqn; Special Duties Flt; Special Duty Flt; Special Signals Flt; Staff Navigators School (Middle East); Staff Pilot Training Unit; Station Flights – Chivenor, Christchurch, Finningley, Hemswell, Khormaksar, Kunming, Netheravon, St Mawgan and Stradishall; 2nd Tactical Air Force CF/Sqn/ Wing; Tactical Air Force (Burma) Communication Sqn/3rd Tactical Air Force Communication Sqn; Technical Command CF; Telecommunications Flying Unit; Torpedo Bombing School; Torpedo Development Unit; Torpedo Training Flt; Torpedo Training Unit; 1 Torpedo Training Unit; Warwick Training Unit; Wellington Conversion Flt; Wellington Flt; 235 Wing; 247 Wing; 334 Wing; 34 Wing Support Unit and Wireless (Intelligence) Development Unit.

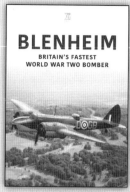

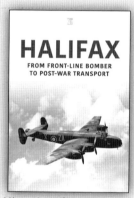

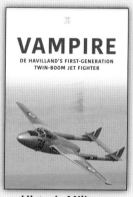